Lose Weight, Find Love, De-Clutter & Save Money

ESSAYS ON HAPPIER LIVING

Michele Woodward

Copyright © 2008 Michele Woodward
All rights reserved.
ISBN: 1-4196-8716-6
ISBN-13: 9781419687167
Visit www.booksurge.com to order additional copies.

for
Munroe & Grace
who teach me so well
every day

Acknowledgements

Like a Hollywood statuette recipient, I have so many people to thank – let's hope I can get them all in before the music starts to swell and some lanky lass attempts to pull me off stage.

I owe a great debt of appreciation to Kay Turley, the woman who finally taught me the difference between a noun and a verb. Kay taught me both in class and out of class, providing books from her own library and thoughts from her own mind that served to open my pea-sized little high school brain to the larger world.

I have been so privileged to have the support of a strong coterie of incredible women through my career. Thanks especially to the wise and kind Anne Wexler; the accepting and empathetic Dr. Mary O'Farrell; and, the smart and inclusive Dr. Martha Beck.

Thanks to Chris Marlow at Innovative Identity and Sally Geidrys, editor extraordinaire, for your help during this book's birthing process.

Thanks to my posse of pals who pushed and prodded and supported me while I languished and anguished about this book: Debra Cavanaugh, Susan Ross, Martha Schlager, Betsey Kirkemo and Fran Wetzel. And thanks too, to my big boosters and dear friends Olivia Gagnon and Joe Munroe. My brother David Tourtellotte has proven time and time again what a blessing he is to my life. All of these people show that family is made up of those we choose to love, as well as those we are born to love.

This book wouldn't have come together without the support of readers who like what I write, so thanks to all of you faithful readers for your continuing support.

Finally, thanks to all of my clients over the years who have taught me as much as or even more than I've ever taught them. It's a pleasure and a privilege to work with you.

Table Of Contents

Introduction 1
Procrastinate...Later 3
Forgiveness 9
Finding Joy 17
The Best Job Interview Question Ever 23
Getting Back To Work 27
Life Is An Experiment 35
The $23 Billion Monkey 41
Saying Goodbye 47
How To Like What You Do 51
When To Quit 57
Ya Gotta Wanna 63
Fight or Flight? Or, Mend and Tend? 69
The Art of Being Lazy 75
Lose Weight, Find Love, De-Clutter and Save Money 79
Doing Enough? 83
Internal Stress 89
Clarity of Purpose 93
Mind Your Own Business 101
In-Box Management 107
Either/Or 113
The Absence of Perfect 119
Authentically You 123
Supply & Demand 129
I Am, I Said 135

The Company You Keep 139
Need More Time? 145
Life's Little Aggravations 151
The Way of Transition 157
When Times Are Tough 163
Risky Business 169
Cleaning A Closet 175
The Difference Between Men and Women 179
A Peaceful, Easy Feeling 185
Standard Operating Procedure 191
Here, But Not Here 197
Whelmed 203

Introduction

When I was a girl, I'd lock myself up for hours, writing. I wrote Nancy Drew-style mysteries. At age 10 I went through a very odd haiku-on-onion-skin-paper phase. In my teen years I wrote overwrought, deeply sensitive poetry as well as witty, goofy letters to friends far away.

As I grew older and grew up, I wrote less and less. Sure, I wrote memos and reports and scintillating emails – as well as notes to teachers, explaining the antics of my own children. But nothing I was very passionate about.

When I started coaching, I began reconnecting people with a lost or forgotten part of themselves. Through that process, I realized that I had to reconnect with the lost writer within me in order to be my very best self.

The essays in this book were born as I reclaimed my writing self. Originally appearing in a weekly newsletter, then a blog over the last several years, I wouldn't have thought there would be any kind of central theme. But, of course, I was wrong! The essays cover themes about reconnecting with yourself; knowing yourself; loving yourself; loving others. What it means to be clear about strengths and weaknesses. How you can make small changes that have huge impact on the quality of happiness in your life.

Introduction

So, this book is ultimately about Happiness. Read one essay at a time, read them all at one sitting – hey, it's your book! And when you're through, it's my hope that you'll be a little bit clearer, a little bit more forgiving, a little bit more open, and a whole lot happier.

PROCRASTINATE...LATER

People certainly beat themselves up for procrastinating. Well, when they get around to it, they beat themselves up.

But what if procrastinating wasn't that bad? Just think: what if procrastination could actually be good for you?

Example One: You procrastinate about buying that house you toured with your spouse. And three months later, the price has dropped significantly so you buy it at a great savings.

Example Two: You procrastinate about writing that report the boss talked about. And the day before it's due, information comes out that changes the entire strategy — making your report irrelevant.

Example Three: You procrastinate about having that difficult conversation with your co-worker, only to have her come in and apologize — and accept responsibility for her actions.

Sure, you could come up with plenty of examples where procrastination can hurt you, like ignoring those stabbing sharp pains on your lower right side ("It's probably just gas, not appendicitis") and ending up with emergency surgery. Granted.

But when you take a look at why you're procrastinating, you can determine whether it's the right thing to do or not.

When you evaluate The Why, you need to consider how you feel about the decision or task at hand. So, sit with it for a minute. How would it feel to own that house? Scary? Too expensive? Is that why you're procrastinating? In this case, procrastination is sending you information — this house is overpriced. Yay, procrastination!

Sometimes procrastination is a sign that we really don't want to do something. This happens when someone else forces their will on you — remember when your mother ordered you to clean your room, even though it looked fine to you? When you feel you have no control, you might procrastinate in a slightly passive-aggressive way ("I don't wanna, and I'm not gonna") until you provoke a fight that unleashes all your fury and anger. Cue the slamming door portion of the program.

But you might also procrastinate because you need time to collect your thoughts and make your plans. Planning People may appear to be "last-minute" when they've really been working out the problem in their head for some time. This is the way I write, as a matter of fact. I compose in my noggin all week, then sit down to write in one fell swoop.

Seems to work.

One other reason folks can procrastinate is possibly the most difficult to be aware of — they procrastinate so they can get out of their own way. These are our friends The Perfectionists.

Perfectionists can't help themselves. They add, or take away, or refine, or fiddle, or tweak. The more time they have, the more they tinker. I once saw a time-elapse film of Picasso creating a painting. There was a point at which he could have stopped and had a masterpiece. But he kept on fiddling and adding. And ended up with a ruined canvas.

When perfectionists learn to get out of their own way by giving themselves less time, rather than more time, they can deliver a more perfect product. Then they have to deal with what might have been if they really had enough time to do it right.

But that's a different column.

Procrastinating might be central to the way you function in the world, and, if that's so, then embrace it. Use it for good. If procrastinating hurts you, or keeps you from fully enjoying your life, then you might spend more time examining exactly why you keep putting things off. Because once you understand that, you understand yourself. Which is central to living a happy life.

Forgiveness

I WAS A GUEST SPEAKER AT A BOOK CLUB THE OTHER NIGHT — reviewing the best of parenting, relationship and personal growth books – when I was asked, "What about forgiveness?" In response, I talked about the ideas in Dr. Janis Abrahms Spring's book *How Can I Forgive You?*, but as I drove home I felt unsatisfied with my response. It wasn't complete enough.

Don't get me wrong. Dr. Spring's book is terrific, providing a workable framework for moving to forgiveness. It's practical, it's pragmatic and it's well-written. The book was not my problem. I was glad I had mentioned such a useful book.

No, my problem was – no surprise for this "words girl" – the semantics of the word "forgiveness". What is it? What does it mean? We hear about forgiveness from pulpits and pop culture all the time. Why, it's a gift we give ourselves! It's the right thing to do! Forgiving is a sign of our spiritual development and piety!

Forgiveness has become such a ubiquitous word, in fact, that perhaps it's lost its potency. I bump into someone in a crowded store and I say, "Excuse me." Am I asking forgiveness for my offense? Many of us say "sorry" almost as often as we say "uhm". Do we seek forgiveness each time we blurt it out? Teens say, "My bad" and their buds say, "No problem." Is that a forgiveness exchange?

Forgiveness

What does "forgiveness" mean?

As I drove home, pondering, this definition popped into my head:

"Forgiveness is when the hurt you've suffered no longer drives your decision-making, nor defines who you are. "

Here's an example: Tom's wife left him for another man. Tom was devastated. For the first few months, he was among the walking wounded and would tell the story of his betrayal to anyone who'd listen. And some who didn't want to listen. His mind was filled with thoughts of retribution, retaliation and revenge. Nearly every thought he had, nearly every course of action, was directed by his wife's affair and their subsequent divorce. And women? Pffffft. Since his wife had betrayed him and she was a woman, then all women were capable of betrayal and should be avoided. Women were not to be trusted. No one was to be trusted.

He was not in a place of forgiveness.

Over time, though, he began to add different activities to his schedule. He got into mountain biking, planned outings with friends and explored his beliefs. He recommitted himself to his work, and got a promotion. He gingerly made friendships, then dates, with women. Gradually, his decisions were based on his life now, not his life then. He no longer needed to tell the story of his wife's affair to people – because it no longer seemed that relevant. If you asked him, he'd say, "I'm Tom. I'm a 45 year old engineer who likes mountain biking, wine and hanging with friends. Oh, and I'm divorced."

He had arrived at the place of forgiveness.

That doesn't mean his wife's affair had no impact on Tom's life. It did. Forgiveness didn't mean Tom pretended he wasn't hurt. He was. It doesn't mean it was OK for Tom's wife to have had an affair. It wasn't. What happened in his marriage became a part of the accumulated experiences of Tom's life – just not the key, defining part of his life.

Forgiveness meant that Tom was no longer driven or defined by his hurt.

In many cases, one person hurts another person and they stay in a relationship. The hurt may be big or it may be small. But it's a hurt and the only way forward is through forgiveness. This mutual forgiveness benefits both parties.

We've seen how a hurt person's path to forgiveness helped him. In an ongoing relationship, forgiveness is a huge relief for the injuring party, too. She knows that she's not going to "have to pay for this for the rest of my life" since his decisions are not going to be solely based on the hurt ("I'm only doing this because you lied to me twenty-five years ago."). And she knows he's not going to forever define her by having hurt him ("You know I can't trust you because you lied to me that time twenty-five years ago."). But to get to forgiveness she has do her part. She has to acknowledge that he's been hurt, she has to work to help him recover, and she has to promise not to willfully repeat the injury in the future.

Sometimes the person who needs forgiveness is you. Many people, for instance, carry shame and guilt over a failed marriage, or a lost job, or a blown diet. "If only I had…If only I had been…If only I hadn't…" is a constant refrain. Yet, this song is an oldie. It has a good beat, and you can dance to it. But it's the same old song and dance. Singing it keeps us firmly in the past. When where we've got to live is in the now.

Forgiving ourselves – acknowledging what happened, how it impacted us then and now – and moving to the point where our perceived shortcomings no longer fuel our decision-making or define who we are, is the key to living in the present. And living happily. This may require therapy to understand how we hurt ourselves in the past and to work through the issues so that we don't continue to hurt ourselves in the future.

Viktor Frankl, noted psychiatrist and author of the classic *Man's Search for Meaning*, founded an innovative school of psychology called "logotherapy", which holds that if people have meaning and conscience in their lives then they are more apt to be successful. This idea underpins much of modern psychological thought and took mental health into new and productive areas.

Now for the reveal. Frankl developed his theories while imprisoned in Auschwitz. *Man's Search for Meaning* details the suffering, deprivation and humiliation the men and women in the camp endured. It was unlike anything most of us have seen. No one should experience such inhumanity.

Although Frankl's experience in Auschwitz birthed the most significant work of his life, Frankl didn't appear to define himself by the time in the camp – rather, he defined himself by his work, his life.

He became bigger than what he had suffered.

And that's the promise of forgiveness. You can become bigger than your hurt. With forgiveness you can leave the wound in the past and be your best self. And you can start right now.

Finding Joy

Are you happy? Is there joy in your life?

It is so hard for some folks to find joy. Maybe they think they aren't entitled, or they have the feeling that it's somehow inappropriate. It's as if once you become a grown up you must put your shoulder to the wheel, nose to the grindstone keeping a stiff upper lip, and suffer through the rest of your life. Happiness is for the indolent or the indulgent. It's silent suffering for the rest of us.

Ah, the good old Puritan Work Ethic.

I am here to tell you that it is possible to have both work and joy. It's possible to have a balance between the two, in a perfect Joy/Work ratio. If you don't have enough joy in your life, your Joy/Work ratio might be out of balance. Here are just a few things you can do today to right the scales.

1. Figure out what brings you joy. Do you know how many people have to think about what brings them joy? Plenty, that's how many. So take a little inventory. Do you find joy with people, or with things? In certain places? With certain aromas? When do you feel joy? As long as it's legal and doesn't hurt anyone else, you are good to go.

2. Be conscious of opportunities for joy. The Buddhists practice "mindfulness", which includes being aware of one's surroundings and interactions. In my own life,

I realized I got great joy out of the way light plays on living plants and trees. So, I take time to look at the backlit leaves of the red maple outside my office window. I find myself driving or walking and noting the color of tulips, or the pink of the dogwood, or the earthy brown of a moldering tree. And I feel very, very joyful. Be aware of what brings you to that place of joy and be mindful of opportunities to express it.

3. Make time for joy. Once you figure out what brings you true joy, whether it's having deep conversations with friends, or watching a baseball fly out of the park, fair, on a summer afternoon, or digging in the dirt, or painting, or yoga, or love – make time for it. Don't put off your joy until tomorrow, you Puritan you. Tomorrow, as we have all learned by now, may not come the way we think it will.

4. Express gratitude. It's been said that it's impossible to feel both sad and grateful at the same time. Remind yourself just how grateful you are. Then, tell people you value them, journal your grateful thoughts, live in a perpetual state of gratitude. Joy will ensue.

When I was a child, I was enamored of a Hanna-Barbera show – the animated "Gulliver's Travels." One of the Lilliputians was a rotund little doom-and-gloom guy whose stock catchphrase was "We're doomed. We'll never make it." Although I've been know to have used this exact catchphrase myself from time to time, I've come to figure out that predicting doom usually insures it. I now avoid such predictions at all costs, and seek out the joy in a situation.

There is almost always some joy, somewhere. Real joy is so… joyful. It's that unbearable lightness of being. It's like bubbles in good champagne. It's in a baby's belly laugh. Dare I say it? Joy is happiness, distilled in a moment.

Yep, I used the H-word. Happiness. Don't be frightened of the idea of being happy. Happiness is good. Happiness can change your life.

Dr. Jon Haidt, noted researcher at the University of Virginia and author of *The Happiness Hypothesis*, suggests that the H-word can be rendered in the following formula: $H = S + C + V$. "S" is your set point – whether you see the glass half empty or half full. "C" stands for the conditions of your life – a long commute, a disability, poverty. "V" covers your voluntary activities, or those things you choose to do: to volunteer, to take a class, to make changes in your life.

To make the quickest jump in H, you can focus on your C and your V. But to dramatically shift the texture and tenor of your life, attack your S. Learning to see the glass as half full, regardless of the circumstances, will profoundly raise your H.

Unabashedly welcome joy into your life. It'll make you happy.

The Best Job Interview Question Ever

So, you've made it through the first round of interviews for that new position. Now it's the second – or third – round. "Tell me a little about yourself" has been asked. Maybe you've even been asked, "If you were a tree, what kind of tree would you be?" You know, all the important stuff.

Remember that job interviews are not only your opportunity to "sell" yourself, but are your chance to evaluate whether the job is actually something you'll like and be good at. To figure that out, you have to do more than give the right answer to questions – you also have to <u>ask</u> the right questions.

To that end, I've come up with The Best Job Interview Question Ever. And it has nothing whatsoever to do with trees.

Ready? Here it is:

"What's the first task you'd like me to accomplish in this job?"

Whether you're interviewing for a CEO position or a job on the loading dock, the beauty of this question is multi-fold.

If everyone you interview with responds with "We need you to streamline our HR processes and make sure we're in compliance with OSHA guidelines", you can be certain that the organization is clear on what the job is about.

But, if the guy in accounting says, "You need to clear up the spreadsheets", and the woman in marketing says, "You have to make new collateral materials", and the CEO says, "We're looking for someone to clean house", and the gal in sales says, "I have no idea what you're here for," you've got a problem. The organization may be disorganized, lack leadership or not function well as a team. Here's what you do in this situation: exit, quickly, stage left.

When you ask The Best Question, you might find that the expectations expressed are completely unrealistic. "I want you to drive up share prices by 50%, reduce the workforce by 30%, acquire companies more profitable than we are, and find the Holy Grail." Again, this is your tip-off that the job may not be right for you. Or for anyone.

Having a clear sense of organizational priorities allows you to snag what writer Michael Watkins calls an "early win." His book *The First 90 Days* has great advice on making the most of a new job – in short, when you meet or exceed expectations early, you are guaranteed success.

The interview process is fraught with anxiety and stress – but discovering how your colleagues and bosses will judge you as a winner before you take the job is a surefire way to insure you have less stress and more success.

∽

Getting Back to Work

Show me a woman 40 to 55 years old who's been home with her kids, and I'll bet you she's had this thought at one point or the other: "Maybe I should go back to work." And with the magic of my all-knowing, all-seeing swami-like brainpower, I'll bet she's also said, "Who'd hire someone like me, who's gone 15 years without a pay check?"

It's not that I'm able to read minds. I usually can't. Rather, I am able to listen, and plenty of women are talking about how to transition back to work.

As a coach, I've been able to successfully help at-home moms find their way back meaningful and lucrative employment. Want to know how?

Know what you're good at, and what you like to do. Just because you worked 70 hours a week as a partner in a law firm, doesn't mean you have to do that now. Many former highly skilled women forecast ahead and see a very black or white future, when it comes to going back to work. "I have to go back as a full-time partner or I can't go back at all." Not so, grasshopper. You are smarter and wiser than you were then. Just make an inventory of what was best about what you did in your job, and add in the things you like about what you're doing now. There may be similarities, or eye-popping opportunities that arise from a crosshatch of your past and your present.

The gap won't matter to people who know what you can do. Over 70% of jobs are filled by personal referral, so rely on your network of contacts — both from your professional days and from your at-home days. Let's say you were a ferocious litigator who became a ferocious advocate for diversity in your children's school. Perhaps you could go to a non-profit dedicated to diversity and offer your services. They might not need you full-time, but they might help you find your Bridge Job.

Love the beauty of the "Bridge Job". The beauty of what I call the "Bridge Job" is that it's often short-term, project-oriented, working for someone who knows you and has a specific need. Often the Bridge Job is just a means to an end — with the end being your next job. I recently coached a wonderful woman whose Bridge Job was in the Federal Government, working for a former boss. This position gave her a perch from which she could do good work, build her network, establish a salary level and get her self-confidence. I am pleased to announce that she recently left the government for a big, hot-shot job on Wall Street.

There was a time when I was a full-time mom, at home with my wonderful kids. Although I enjoyed my time in corporate America, and truly loved working at the White House, mothering my children was just about the best experience I ever had. But like a lot of women, at a certain point time and events collided, so I went back to work.

In some ways, I took an easy path — I re-started my consulting/coaching practice. And starting a business that reflects your own values can be an excellent way to go forward. I am coaching several woman-owned small businesses as they grow and develop — and watching the institutionalization of things like flexibility and Bridge Jobs and openness is truly inspiring.

I am also coaching women who are taking the harder path: re-entering the corporate workplace. Their big fears? Who will hire someone with an "employment gap"? If they do get a job, will they have to work 70 hour weeks? Will they have flexibility? Will they have seniority?

Fortunately, the picture is beginning to shift for women re-entering the workforce. Sylvia Hewlett's new book *Off-Ramps and On-Ramps: Keeping Talented Women On The Road To Success* (Harvard Business School Press), provides an excellent template for corporations and organizations to follow to ease the non-linear careers of women.

Attention all HR executives, recruiters and C-level folks who read this blog (and there are many of you): You need to get this book and take a long, hard look at the realities hiring futurists predict. Disqualifying candidates simply because they took time off to care for children, or elders, or their own health, eliminates a talented and vital portion of highly qualified individuals. Developing innovative ways to recruit, retain and support these people may just be the key to your long-term business success.

What Hewlett calls "The White Male Career Model"— continuous, goal-oriented movement; full time employment and office face time; 'catching the wave' of a big promotion in your 30s; primarily motivated by money — is falling by the wayside. I wrote about the differences between men and women a few weeks ago. If you recall, I suggested men are goal-oriented and women are experience-oriented in many aspects of life. Hewlett supports this idea with research that shows women — regardless of whether they have children or not — are more motivated by the connections they make in their work, and balance, than in monetary rewards. "The Female Career Model" then, would include nonlinear careers; a mix of full/part-time/project work; an ability to pass up promotions selectively; a focus on connections and experience over money. Hewlett's research shows that women really want to 'give back' in their work — and be fairly compensated, naturally. But waving more money in front of a woman to get her to comport to the White Male Career Model is going to be an attempt that fails.

What she needs, and values, is connection, flexibility, and a culture that drops the stigma surrounding 'dropping out' or 'cutting back'.

Before I close, I want to tell you about a friend of mine who worked in politics and government. She was a very successful and well-regarded human resources executive. Then she married (a great guy) and they had children. My friend stepped back from her work and became an at-home mother. After the disputed 2000 election, she was called to "help" with the mountains of personnel paperwork piling up. It was a short-term position that ended up going something like 18 months. She went back to mothering. Then, she was approached about taking a big, full time job in the government, which she did. She called me one day and said, "Anyone can do this, Michele. It's not hard. You don't lose your skills — it all comes back!" Today, this friend of mine serves as one of the highest ranking women in the White House — she's Anita McBride, former at-home mom, now Chief of Staff to the First Lady.

You can go back to work after a gap in your employment history. It's possible. Target people who know you, and know what you can do. Aim for a Bridge Job as you transition from one stage of your life to another. Select people and organizations who prize flexibility and other values important to you.

And, remember what Anita said, "You don't lose your skills — it all comes back!"

Life Is An Experiment

It has been brought to my attention that "deciding" is a subject that needs discussion. Deciding — making a choice or a judgment about something — can carry such overwhelming heavy freight that it seems so much easier to decide...not to decide.

Not doing anything, though, can prolong pain, suffering and unhappiness. In not deciding, friends, you stay firmly stuck.

So how do you make good decisions?

First, allow yourself this idea: Life Is An Experiment. When you're stuck, viewing yourself as a scientist who applies the scientific method to her hypotheses can give you a little room in which to move.

In the scientific method, you first make an observation and generate a hypothesis about what you observe. Then you come up with a predictable, rigorous way to challenge the hypothesis and you test it. If the data you collect in the test doesn't support the original hypothesis, you get to change your underlying thought — and maybe move out of stuck.

Here's an example: A 14 year old guy at his first high school dance has this tightly held belief that no girl would possibly dance with him. He's never actually asked anyone to dance, mind you, but jumped right to a hypothesis, based on narrow observations of himself as a guy who is a little too skinny, or too fat, or too pimply, or too dorky. He thinks he's not quite right in so many ways, so he assumes all girls share his observations (many of us make this leap, so let's not be too hard on the lad).

Now, to test the hypothesis that no girl will dance with him: what can he do?

Why, he can ask a girl to dance.

My simple guideline is to test the hypothesis three times. So our young man needs to ask three girls to dance.

In his mind, as a scientist, he's not opening himself to three bouts of rejection. No, sirree. He's merely collecting three data points. Doesn't that feel easier?

If one girl says "yes", and one girl says "no", then his results are inconclusive. It's when he asks the third girl that his hypothesis is either proved or disproved.

But either way, look at what happened: he actually asked someone to dance. Regardless of whether Girl #3 dances or sits like a lump on a folding chair in the corner, our young man has actually put himself out there and done something he previously considered impossible. Just one girl saying "yes" tells him what's possible.

When you face an obstacle in your own life and your hypothesis is something like "this will never work", try the scientific method. Observe. Make a hypothesis. Construct a challenging test of your theory. Test it. Look at the results and change your theory if you need to.

When you view life as an experiment in which you simply collect data points, there is very little that needs to be perfect. You are just conducting tests that provide you with information you need to go forward.

Think of the hypotheses that may govern your life: "I can't lose weight", or "No one would hire me", or "I'm too old to find a new job", "I can't tell my mother how I really feel" — and apply the scientific method.

Perhaps in the testing of your hypothesis you will find that the data don't truly support your thinking. It's simply your thinking that needs to change.

And then you'll be unstuck.

∽

THE $23 BILLION MONKEY

I was watching a hockey game the other day when I overhead a little girl ask her mother, "What happens if nobody wins?" And with a shrug, the mother answered, "Somebody always wins, honey." Which got me thinking.

A la Jerry Seinfeld, what's the deal with winning? There's always got to be a winner, whether in sports, politics – even merging into traffic. Why does winning hold so much power for human beings? Especially humans of the dude variety. Ever notice that interest in professional sports rose as the opportunities for men to go to war decreased? I'm just sayin'...

Winning is held in such esteem that a tie, where there is no clear victor, leads to "sudden death." As in, the battlefield death of the vanquished. Would it be different if we called the tie-breaking overtime outcome "sudden victory"? Feels much less satisfying, no?

Earlier in the week I spoke with a man who is considering starting his own business in an industry he knows extremely well. We discussed the competitive landscape and he noted that the industry leader is known for cut-throat tactics and a lack of integrity. "I don't want my company to be like that," he said. "But, can I be successful if I'm not number one?"

Author and tech marketing guru Geoffrey Moore says you can, if you're smart. He says there are three different kinds of players in a competitive market: Gorillas, Chimps and Monkeys.

Gorillas are the segment leaders, whose products become the industry standard. Think Coca-Cola. Chimps are the challengers – think Pepsi. And Monkeys are the guys who follow along in the market, aping the Gorillas and Chimps, often positioning themselves as unique or offering excellent customer service to get business. Think Cadbury-Schweppes.

In business as in sports, we think we have to be a Gorilla to be successful. But monkeys can make great businesses. Sure, Coke's market cap is nearly $137 billion, but Schweppes? There are plenty of bubbles in ginger ale, friends — $23 BILLION worth of bubbles.

And you can't tell me that ain't a successful business.

"Winning's not everything, it's the only thing," said legendary coach Vince Lombardi. Uh huh. Guess it depends on how you define winning. Because being Number Three, the $23 billion dollar Monkey, can be extremely satisfying. Considering the energy needed to maintain Gorilla status, being a Monkey – doing what you love and doing it well, sounds pretty appealing.

Pressuring yourself to always be the winner can lead to incredible stress. And, as the New England Patriots proved, nobody wins all the time. Some of the best learning I ever had, in fact, was working on a losing Presidential campaign. Sure, winning would have been great – but I learned how to handle defeat somewhat gracefully. I learned about what works, and what doesn't, in campaigns. I learned about loyalty, and friendship. I learned just how far I can be pushed, physically, emotionally and mentally. I learned about what's really important.

Which is worth the market capitalization of Coca-Cola to me.

The next time you find yourself driving yourself (or your kids, or your work group, or your spouse) to be the Gorilla, ask yourself this: Is winning worth being completely stressed out? What's to be learned from doing my absolute best, even if I'm not the Gorilla? Can I be content with being a very successful, centered, happy Monkey?

I say: pass the bananas, baby, 'cuz the world needs more happy monkeys.

༄

It's hard to say goodbye. As Shakespeare so aptly put it, "Parting is such sweet sorrow." And in this life there is much to be parted from, often with much grief.

One man becomes suddenly, critically ill and must part with the idea of his youth and vigor.

One young mother loses her own mother, and must part with the idea of herself as someone's beloved child.

One man parts with his wedding ring after his wife's death, and lets go of the idea of himself as someone's husband.

One woman parts with her home and possessions and adjusts to the idea that she won't live independently for the rest of her life.

I've written about crisis and how it can change lives. Crisis forces a redefinition of who we are, and what's important to us. Altering those fundamental views about ourselves is, no surprise, life changing.

Catalytic crisis requires us to move from the cocoon of "known-self" to "unknown-self". Embracing the unknown is not something many of us handle particularly well… so, in the alternative, we cling fearfully, ferociously to our known-self.

Known-self may have worked for years. We're comfortable with all the rules in known-self – and we can anticipate with confidence how we and others will act. Even if we know we're unhappy in our known-self, at least we know what to expect! Who wants to upset the apple cart? But when clinging to known-self feels like pain, you will change it. Sometimes it seems it takes a crisis to show us just how ill-fitting known-self has become.

The prospect of unknown-self is murky, and for those with control issues, it's precisely the unknowing that's so hard. Parting with a definition that really doesn't work should be, on its face, easy to do. However, parting with the known in favor of the unknown – that seems scary. It's like emerging from the cocoon we've constructed as a worm and learning to live as a butterfly. None of the old rules seem to apply.

So, in those moments, remember: "parting is such <u>sweet</u> sorrow."

When you say goodbye to something old that no longer fits, you open space for something new. It's the opportunity for "new-self". Which could be something nicer, better, happier. Could be something that helps you live more fully. Could be something sweet.

Be open to the opportunity for change that life brings. Welcome it. Because it's your chance to flap your butterfly wings… and fly.

How To Like What You Do

Susan's complaining about her job. Oh, no, she likes her work – she's just not crazy about the people she's working with. She's in a high-pressure, high-performance field where you "eat what you kill" – in other words, she's paid a percentage of the contracts she closes.

The more we talk, it's apparent that Susan's frustrated because no one in the office is interested in working on projects with anyone else. No one refers Susan clients. No one comes to the parties she throws. People poach each other's support staff. She's never worked in a place like this and she's thinking about leaving.

I recommended Susan take the Myers-Briggs assessment. "But that's just for teams!" she blurted. "What can it do for an individual?" [note blatant set up here, which neatly introduces the subject I really want to write about!]

Back in the early 1920s, Katharine Cook Briggs discovered the work of pioneering psychologist Carl Jung. Katharine had been doing her own independent research on personality – hoping to devise a tool to identify personality differences so that people could understand themselves and others – and in Jung's theories found a workable personality type framework.

Katharine, the daughter of a college professor, had been home-schooled, so she home-schooled her own daughter,

Isabel, in the same manner. In time, Isabel Briggs Myers – armed with just a bachelor's degree, her mother's insights and her own determined curiosity – developed the Myers-Briggs Type Indicator (MBTI).

I love the idea that a mother and her daughter, working together, developed such a useful and insightful tool. They encountered resistance from the academic community who scoffed at their indicator – they had no training, no credentials! Who did these women think they were?!

Katharine and Isabel, mother and daughter, weathered that storm. Eighty-some years after Katharine began her research, the Myers-Briggs Type Indicator is the the most widely used personality assessment in the world.

You may have taken the MBTI at some point – and found your personality type represented by four letters, E or I, S or N, T or F, P or J. Sound at all familiar? There are sixteen possible combinations. You have a preference for either Extroversion or Introversion. You either Sense or Intuit. You Think or you Feel. You Perceive or you Judge.

"But," you say with a tiny whimper, "I am both Extroverted and Introverted. It depends on the situation." You are absolutely right. Jung theorized that, at our best, we know when it's appropriate to be Introverted and Extroverted, to Sense or to Intuit, and so on. The MBTI gets to what our innate preference is, regardless of which we may use in a particular situation.

Let's try an example of preference. Cross your arms across your chest. Note which arm is on top. Now, switch your arms so that the top arm is on the bottom. How's that feel?

Awkward? Bet so. You have a marked preference for how you cross your arms, just as you have marked preferences for the way you see the world.

Neat, huh?

People with particular preferences tend to cluster in the same kind of field. Studies have shown, for instance, that people who choose the military have similar personality types – hierarchical, traditional, practical – and that makes sense, doesn't it? Similarly, people in the nursing field tend to have similar personality characteristics – concerned with people, empathetic, open to solutions. Each type brings its own strengths and shortcomings, which naturally lend themselves to success or difficulty in particular fields.

After she took the Myers-Briggs assessment, I pointed out to Susan that one of the main problems might be that her type (ESFJ) has a strong preference for belonging. It's important that she feel part of a team, that she work in a hierarchy with known roles and an objective system for promotion. That means she might not fit in with an organization that values and rewards autonomous lone wolves. To be happier in her career, she can 1) bring more belongingness into her current workplace, or 2) find a workplace that fosters belonging.

Her eyes opened with understanding, and her path forward became a little clearer. And that's what Myers-Briggs is all about. Understanding yourself, and understanding those around you, so that you can be more effective and clear. Sure, MBTI is great for teams – and [shameless self-plug warning] I'm happy to come into your workplace to deliver a knockout program that will help your team become more efficient, communicate better, solve interpersonal problems and retain employees – but simply knowing and understanding your own personality type, and how it shapes your joys and your struggles, can be an eye-opening experience.

When To Quit

Every once in a while I have one of those weeks where it seems that every client is talking about the same thing. When that happens, I figure I'm getting some big old honking message.

And I have to write about it.

This week, the ubiqui-topic was "When do I quit?" And there seems to be variety in what it is people want to quit – quit smoking, quit a job, quit a relationship, quit worrying.

But how do you know it's time? How can you be sure you're clear, and leaving for the right reasons? What are the right reasons, anyway?

It's time to quit when the person you are becoming is someone you don't like. When you're in a job, and as a condition of employment you are expected to fudge facts, shift numbers and lie to customers, you become a person who fudges, shifts and lies. Is that who you want to be?

A relationship that asks you to set aside your own personal goals, your own friends, your own hobbies – that asks you to nag, or to make excuses for another person, or to change your beliefs – who are you in that kind of relationship? You're a person with no rudder. You're a person with no self. Is that who you want to be?

When To Quit

It's time to quit when you find that you love having the problem more than the problem loves you. If you find yourself talking about the problem all the time, stewing and fretting, worrying about it, analyzing it, turning the problem over and over in your head – is that who you want to be? Is that how you want to use your energy?

There's an underlying ubiqui-thought we need to address, friends, and it's: "I should be able to make this work."

Maybe you could make it work. If you were King of The Forest and could control all the elements. So, let me ask you – do you control your boss? Can you stop him from giving you an ASAP assignment – at 5pm on New Year's Eve? Can you stop him from lobbing f-bombs at you? Can you stop her from excluding you from important meetings, or distribution of key memos?

Can you make your boyfriend sober? Can you single-handedly restore your spouse to mental health? Is it possible to string together the perfect set of words that will make your boss sit up and say, "By golly, you're absolutely right! I'm a jerk! I am going to change 30 years of my behavior just because of what you said!"

Ah, folks can dream. But we know the truth: you only control yourself, and you only change yourself. "Making this work" often means adapting yourself to something that's unhealthy.

And you become, over time, someone you don't want to be.

"Yes, but…" is another tactic we use to stay stuck in an unhealthy situation. "Yes, but… when he leaves his wife, stops drinking, goes to counseling and gets a job, everything will be perfect." OK. But for now, he's with his wife, drinking, avoiding counseling and unemployed. That's what's real. The "Yes, but…" you're waiting for might never happen.

And who are you becoming while you wait?

You and only you have the opportunity, and the right, to live the life you are meant to live. Quitting that which is unhealthy for you and moving toward that which is healthy can be really, really hard. But it's the only way you become someone you really, really like.

༄

Ya Gotta Wanna

CONSIDERING MAKING SOME CHANGES HERE AT THE END OF ONE year and the start of a brand spanking new one? Gonna lose weight? Stick to your budget? Change jobs? Travel to Bali? Find yourself that elusive soul mate?

Sure every year you make resolutions; but this year, by golly, you're really gonna do it.

Well, all I'm gonna say is, "Ya gotta wanna."

How many times have you found yourself in late December writing down the New Year's Resolution to Get Into Better Shape, and by February you find yourself couch potato sluggish – not going to the gym you paid for, or even using those getting-dusty weights in the back of the closet?

My guess? You didn't really wanna get into shape.

Because if you did really wanna, you woulda.

The sneaky sabotage comes into play when we say one thing yet do another. We say we want to pay off our credit card debt yet we continually splurge on something we "deserve", or that makes us "feel better". Result? We end the year with two additional credit cards, and everything maxed out.

And we feel like a failure.

Which is, of course, why we didn't pay off the credit card in the first place.

Doing Enough?

When you feel like a failure, you create opportunities to remind yourself that you are, indeed, a failure. What does a failure do? Why, fail! So, you fail to pay your bills on time – and the nastygrams from your creditors reinforce your idea about yourself... that you're a loser. You fail to eat healthy food and moderately exercise, and what happens? Why, you gain weight, lose muscle tone and feel... bleah. But isn't that how a failure is supposed to feel?

To turn this around, there is only one thing you can do. And you gotta wanna. You gotta wanna move from failure to success. Really, really wanna. Ready?

Take out a piece of paper. Oh, and a pen. Or pencil. Or fat crayon. Something handy. OK. List the following categories and leave enough space between them to write four or five things under each. The categories are: Career; Money; Health; Physical Environment (your living conditions); Family/Friends; Significant Other/Romance; Personal Growth (continuing education, spiritual growth, etc.); and, Fun & Recreation.

Focus on what you did, rather than what you didn't. That's a switch, huh?

When you're finished, look at your list of accomplishments for the year. Any patterns? Anything interesting? What's that tell you about your year?

This was a tough year for a client of mine, Susan. A year ago, she lost her senior executive position due to an industry shake-up. Then both parents got ill, and she became their legal custodian. She arranged for their care, took responsibility for finances, coordinated with the extended family. A full-time job – while she was looking for a full-time job. In the last three months, her father died and her sister unexpectedly died – and her mother remains ill.

But.

In the last year, she rekindled friendships. She moved to her dream city. She put lovely things into her new home. She made smart financial decisions. She exercised. She traveled. She continued to expand her professional network. She sought support when she needed it. She took care of herself.

Although Susan might say, "2007 was a lost year", her list would indicate that she actually made some important steps. Sure, she did what she had to. But the things she really, really wanted to do? She got those done, too.

When you shift your thoughts from "look at what a mess I am" to "look at what I've done", you shift your perspective from perpetual loser to resilient achiever. Even if your achievements are small, they are still yours.

"Michele", you say. "What's the point? I only made accomplishments in areas that really don't matter. I still don't have (a partner, a great job, a million dollars)." I, in my most wise Yoda-like way will ask, "Why are you afraid of leaving Loserville and moving into Successville? What's keeping you from claiming all of your power and accomplishments? What benefit do you get from believing that what you do doesn't matter?"

Getting rid of your negative beliefs about yourself is the key to making progress on any New Year's resolutions you may make. Shifting from a sense of limitation and lack to an awareness of opportunities and abundance completely changes your life. Things become more effortless, you become happier. Believe me, it can be done and you can get there.

But ya really gotta wanna.

Fight or Flight? Or, Mend and Tend?

Our cavemen ancestors were pretty wily characters. But they had to be. Their survival depended on it.

They developed an evolved ability to notice changes – because if the T-Rex usually drank at the water hole in the morning, then that might be a safe time to go out and gather berries. If they saw fresh footprints, or droppings, or heard roars outside the cave, that might be a change – and might be the wrong time to poke a nose out of the old cave.

It was good for Grandma and Grandpa Caveman if everything went as expected, because that meant no surprises. No T-Rex coming out of nowhere, looking to eat a clueless Caveman. Yep, Grandma and Grandpa kept an eye out for changes, noted them, then tried to predict how to behave so they wouldn't get eaten.

We modern humans don't like change, either. We resist it. We deny it. We attempt to wish it away. It's just that surprises can be so…surprising. Think about a time you were surprised or startled at something which wasn't what you had expected. Did your heart race? Did your vision tunnel down? Did you have the urge to get the hell out of there?

Why, you're just like a caveman!

This jumble of reactions to being startled or surprised is call "the fight or flight phenomena" and we've all heard about it for ages. But guess what? Like so much other research, the studies which documented fight or flight were done on male subjects. And that's changing. For example, when researchers started doing studies on women and heart disease, they found women had much different heart attack symptoms. Similarly, recent studies at UCLA have shown that women aren't particularly motivated by fight or flight – that's generally a male reaction to stress. Women, rather, stay put – and "mend and tend".

Let me give you an example. There's a war going on. Men are fighting, fleeing, or laying there dying. Women, on the other hand, are Clara Barton or Molly Pitcher. When the workplace is stressful, women often make sure their team has bandages and enough to drink – and this is precisely where women executives get stuck. The war is raging around them and they are oblivious because they are tending to their people.

When I coach women in this situation, I try to reframe "mend and tend" as a uniquely female asset while simultaneously raising women's consciousness that they have to engage in the office politics with the guys. If a woman steps out of the game to tend to her team, she's often "out of it" and excluded as a player, with sometimes devastating career consequences. I think women's basic orientation toward "mend and tend" is the reason so many of us step away from corporate careers and toward our own businesses. It's "The game makes no sense using your rules – I'll play by my own rules, thank you very much."

Dr. Michael Gurian, in his book *What Could He Be Thinking?* talks at length about how men are constantly calibrating their sense of worth by evaluating the men they are around. They 'sportify' nearly all they do, with teams and statistics and standings – just so they can know where they are vis a vis the "other guys". [Sportify is my own word, dontcha like it? Feel free to work it into any conversation you'd like. Hey, wonder if I can get it into Webster's…!]

Bottom line: women are just wired differently than men. To jump to another subject, I think that's why some women are not participating in politics. With all the reportage around who's up, who's down, margin of error – it's sportified to the point that it's not relevant to the way many women see the world. [oh, I just used sportify again! It's starting to catch on!]

While men continue to dominate the executive suites, fight or flight will be the common currency of the leadership class. But it won't always be that way. The women I'm coaching today are the CEOs of tomorrow. I've talked with executive recruiters who are desperate for qualified women to put forward as CEO candidates, and Board of Director candidates. We will shortly have the first woman Speaker of the House – a powerful leadership role a close remove from the Oval Office.

I'll bet you, as more women leaders step into their own unique abilities, we'll see significant change in the way companies work. Because a woman's "mend and tend" approach is a powerful way to build teams, manage groups and create cohesive morale. All things which are vital to success. All things women do quite naturally, thank you very much.

༄

The Art of Being Lazy

All art requires practice, and patience. Art requires the proper setting, too. And there is no better setting to perfect the art of being lazy than summer.

Being truly lazy seems a lost art in our time of instant messaging, instant gratification – instant everything. We enjoy so many luxuries, except the luxury of time, which is precisely what the lazy state of being requires.

Summer beckons us away from the hustle and bustle and toward laziness. To laze about on a summer Sunday means to recharge batteries. To reconnect with other lazy souls. To rest. To think. To meander. To lollygag. To accomplish much, while accomplishing nothing of any great purpose.

And that's the point – to have no apparent point. We spend so much of our working days striving. Summer laziness allows us to deposit that baggage at the door and really relax.

What's funny to me is the number of people who chastise themselves for being "lazy", yet when asked what they've accomplished today, they can tick off ten or twenty things. They don't see lazy as an art, but as a notion anathema to productive living.

But here's the deal: the art of being lazy is just as creative as any other art. While you're being "lazy", you are allowing your fertile mind to grow and bloom. You are creating something new. A new you.

Clarity of Purpose

Lazy is taking a walk – not to get the aerobic workout, but to look at the flowers. Lazy is taking the time to read a book the whole way through – in one sitting. Lazy is a catnap – without giving a hoot about the chores waiting. Lazy is a two hour talk with your teenager about nothing at all, and everything in the world.

Lazy is loving yourself enough to let go of the need to impress and achieve long enough to really and truly relax and recharge.

Being lazy is an art and I mean to be an accomplished practitioner this summer. Will you join me?

Lose Weight,
Find Love,
De-Clutter
and Save Money

Spend an afternoon with the cable remote in your hand and you could come away with the idea that most people in the world are heavier than is healthy, have messy houses, lackluster love lives, and can't save a nickel.

I invested in some couch time the other day (in my on-going effort to perfect The Art of Being Lazy, of course), and was astounded by the number of TV shows about dealing with either too much (like possessions and food) or too little (love, fashion sense). And the one sad common thread among the folks on these shows was their overwhelming feeling of lack and their resulting self-punishing behaviors.

It comes down to this: when we feel powerless, we look to behaviors which allow us to grab onto a little bit of power. If I feel denied love, I am sure-as-shootin' not going to deny myself the cheesecake.

And after I eat the whole cheesecake in one sitting, I feel horrible about myself, decide I'm never going to have a boyfriend and get out of this hellhole of a life, so I turn to the chocolate ice cream in the freezer.

This cycle repeats, spinning down into a not very nice place to be. It's a place of powerlessness.

But there's good news. Turning powerlessness into power is a simple matter of shifting our thoughts. It's going from feeding yourself in an attempt to fill a gap, to feeding yourself out of self-respect and self-love.

It's "I can choose to eat anything, so I am choosing food which tastes good, is good for me and nurtures me."

Baby, that's power.

Power is also saying "I can have any old partner in a New York minute, but to have a partner who respects me and loves me, I have to love and respect myself first." Many of us get involved with unsuitable people because of the thought "Anybody's better than nobody." Anybody, because we maybe chose him out of panic, may be someone who affirms our inner sense of lack, rather than our inner strength. Where's the power in that?

When you chose a partner out of self-respect, you will have a partner worth having. When you spend your money out of self-respect, you will not overspend. When you live with things that reflect your self-respect, your clutter diminishes. When you feed yourself with an eye to nurturing that which is best in you, you will eat healthily.

You have the power to take care of yourself, and eliminate that which holds you back from your best life. You have the power – use it.

Doing Enough?

Raise your hand if you feel like you're not doing enough.

Accomplishments? Nothing major. Rewards? Few. Performance? Not as good as it could be. What still needs to be done? Everything.

If this sounds familiar, then you probably were on the phone with me this week, or buttonholed me at that party Friday night.

It seems so many people look at themselves with utter disappointment. What they do doesn't matter, and if it does matter then talking about it is bragging so... let's not talk about it. No time to rest. No time to reflect. More stuff to do. Got to keep moving.

The problem with this mindset is pretty clear. Thinking this way ratchets your stress level up to 11 on a 10 point scale, and never allows you the satisfaction of a job well done. When there's no satisfaction in what you're doing, there's no way to <u>like</u> what you're doing.

A man has a performance review at work. His supervisor and peers consistently rate his work at 4s and 5s, on a 5 point scale. He, however, rates himself at a 1 or a 2 on all categories. He's mystified at how his co-workers can rate him so high – he doesn't believe them. Don't they know he's a failure? He could be doing so much more.

Doing Enough?

A woman feels she's disappointing her husband because she's not a gourmet cook, and her housekeeping skills are not so hot, especially with the baby in the picture and given her full-time job. She spends a lot of time apologizing. He says there's nothing to apologize about – he loves the food she cooks and thinks she's a wonderful mother. She doesn't believe him. Doesn't he know she's a failure? She could be doing so much more.

Her husband feels he's disappointing her because he's not making as much money as her brother, and he's not as good with a power tool as most men. She tells him she's proud of his work and that power tools aren't that important, that she loves him and he's a good father. He doesn't believe her. Doesn't she know he's a failure? He could be doing so much more.

So whaddya gonna do? Well, let me suggest two things.

First, ask yourself: What will success look like? Put yourself in the successful mindset. What's your life like then? Make a list of all the elements that compose your successful life.

Now, look at your list. How realistic is it? How much is under your direct control? If success looks like taking time to write – you can do that. If success looks like everyone obeying your commands with no argument – you can't do that, sadly, even if you became a dictator. Dictators often die horribly messy deaths in their attempts to squash the thoughts and behaviors of others – and who wants that?

Understand where your unrealistic definitions of success come from ("I want people to obey me because I hate arguments") and, instead of banging your head against the wall, learn some techniques to disagree effectively. You can start with the book *Crucial Conversations* by Patterson, Grenny et al.

Second, take a few minutes to look at what you've really accomplished. At this time of year, I always sit down and write out 20 Things I Have Accomplished This Year. They can be ordinary things like: got the trash to the curb every week. Think that doesn't matter? Hey, what's the alternative? A huge pile of smelly trash spilling out all over your yard? Believe me, getting the trash to the curb matters! As does paying your bills on time, or getting a physical, or a colonoscopy, or training a new employee at the office. Getting through the budget process, or caring for an elderly parent, or making your kid's school lunches – they all matter. And you've accomplished all of them.

But you haven't cured cancer. Or won the Nobel Peace Prize (unless you're Al Gore). OK. But your best friends and closest family would likely give you a prize for all you do for them. Am I right?

My guess is that you are probably doing enough. More than enough. Acknowledging that and giving yourself credit for it can help reduce your stress level. And, taking a hard look at your expectations of success laid next to your actual accomplishments can provide a roadmap for your future success. Your roadmap may show that you need to reallocate your time and attention – and spend more time creating meaningful success and less time wallowing in your perceived failure.

Internal Stress

A HUNDRED YEARS AGO, SOCIETY FROWNED UPON THOSE WHO were left-handed. In fact, the bias against lefties goes back quite a while. The Latin word refering to the left hand, *sinister*, means evil, while the word referring to the right hand, *dexter*, means correct. A hundred years ago schools "broke" lefties and turned them into righties. It's estimated that seven to ten percent of the population is left-handed, so plenty of people were just plain wrong, perhaps even evil, in society's eyes.

Do you struggle with similar internal stress? Plenty of us do. It's being introverted in a family of extroverts. It's being extroverted in a family that expects silence. It's being a gentle soul in a workplace that expects you to be a shark. It's being a shark living in a monastery. It's wanting to live in the woods and paint when you're expected to live in a gated community and be a lawyer. It's wanting to live in a gated community and be a lawyer when everyone in your world values painters who live like Thoreau.

A few years ago I had the incredible opportunity to be at the Smithsonian when they brought out the rare Stradivari, and had virtuoso musicians play them. The sound that came from those ancient instruments! The skill with which they were played!

It seems that every instrument has one note it resonates to – the note that is true and clear. When this note is played, the instrument transcends itself and the musician and creates a wholly new, marvelous thing. Singers, too, have this kind of resonate note. It's the note you sing when someone says, "Sing." It may be sharp or flat, high or low – but it's your natural note. And when you sing it, your soul thrums.

Internal stress comes from having to sing another person's resonant note. You live in constant contradiction with your essential, true self. No thrum. Ever.

If you don't know your own internal resonant note, don't fear. You can find it. You may have repressed it in order to fit in, or, like our left-handed friend, to avoid shame – but, believe me, it's still there inside you. How to find it?

Start by daring to live as your essential self. Be introverted if that's the way you were born. Be loud if that's how you really are. Be a goofball. Be serious. Be sentimental, be generous, be a hopeless romantic – be whatever you are when you're truly, authentically your best self.

When you stop fighting your innate yearning, and just pick up that pencil in your left hand regardless of what people say – you will have found your creative, true self.

To defeat your internal stress, all you have to do is dare to sing your own note.

CLARITY OF PURPOSE

I'VE BEEN RUNNING INTO A LOT OF STRESSED OUT, TENSE PEOPLE recently. They all seem to be singing that old refrain from The Guess Who, "I got, got, got, got no time." And these are women who are at home with their kids! Add in office politics for those attempting to do both career and parenting, and you've got stratospheric stress levels.

Thank goodness you're reading this today. Because this is for you stressed out souls – especially all you people who think asking for help is a sign of weakness. Ahem.

OK, I'll tell you how to live life with no tension, no stress. Lean into your computer screen and pretend I'm whispering this next part, just like Connie Chung.

Know why you're doing what you're doing.

Simple, huh?

Let's look at it in action. In a typical week, Cheryl wakes up two mornings at 3:45am to get two of her kids to swim practice. She's in a carpool so she only drives the kids to the pool one of those mornings. The other morning, she tries to go back to sleep but usually ends up oversleeping and wakes up just as the kids return from the pool. She wakes her third child, scrambles to get everyone fed, lunches made, homework in backpacks, then tears out of the house to make the early

Clarity of Purpose

tutoring sessions scheduled for her kids. She has not showered nor has she had anything to eat.

While the kids are at school, she does laundry, walks the dog, goes to the grocery store, returns library books, shops for her elderly mother, volunteers at the kids' schools (the three of them are in two different schools), and makes phone calls for a fundraiser. At 3pm, she races to school – late, again. One child goes to tennis, one to dance, the other to piano lessons. On Wednesdays, it's karate, basketball and art. At 7pm Cheryl pulls out chicken nuggets and pasta for her kids and they begin two hours of homework. She checks all their work and corrects their mistakes. On Tuesday and Thursday nights the schedule changes when her oldest child has hockey practice. Dinner those nights is from a drive-thru, eaten in the back of the car. Cheryl's husband comes home from work around 8:30pm, except for the nights he's traveling or at his son's hockey games.

At 10 pm, Cheryl gets her kids into bed and falls, half dead, into her own bed. Her husband, a night owl, stays up watching TV or surfing the Internet until 1am. At dawn the next day, it starts all over again.

Sound at all familiar? Should be. Because most of Cheryl's friends are just like her.

Here's something I know to be true: where you put your attention will grow more important in your life. So where is Cheryl's attention? On her kids. And we will all say, " Yep, your kids should be your Number One priority." But friends, there's priority and there's over-focus.

That's why having clarity of purpose is vital to living a happy life. When you read Cheryl's story, what would you say is her priority? To be self-sacrificing, have no life of her own, and do everything for her children? 'Cuz that's what's she's doing. She's not eating, not bathing, not really in much of a relationship with her husband. She's got no time with friends, no hobbies, no passions.

Why would Cheryl do this?

Henri Nouwen, noted spiritual writer, suggested that busyness is our way to quiet the yearnings of our heart. It's often difficult for women to articulate their own needs or passions society sends a strong message that doing so is selfish and not womanly. Cheryl would tell you, after her second glass of wine, that she knows that she keeps busy so she won't have to think about it. "If I look at why I do things, I might have to change something," she'd acknowledge.

And we all know change is scary.

So, Cheryl stays purposefully busy – so she doesn't have to think about what she wants, and nothing has to change. "Most people prefer the certainty of misery to the misery of uncertainty" wrote therapist Virginia Satir. And Cheryl would agree.

When Cheryl coasts, she takes the path of least resistance. She doesn't have to ask her husband to be a partner (he might say no, he might think I'm not capable, he might leave, we might get divorced, what would people think?). She doesn't have to give her children boundaries and limits (they might miss an opportunity to find something they're good at, they might hate me, they might ridicule me, what would people think?). She doesn't allow her children to be independent (it's faster to do it myself, they won't need me, I'll have to get a job, I haven't had a job for 12 years, I have no skills).

Clarity of Purpose

Cheryl's decision tree goes something like this:

If I acknowledge what I feel, people will be mad → they will leave me → I will be all by myself → I will die all alone → I am not good enough for anyone to love → I do not matter.

At the core of many of our actions is this thought: "I am so flawed that no one can possibly love me (I can't even love myself)." So we attempt to cover our "flaws" thinking that if we move fast enough, and produce enough, our flaws are not going to be noticeable. Even to ourselves.

This is where coaching can really help. A good coaching relationship allows all you Cheryls (and Toms and Susans and Harolds) out there to take some time to look at who you are and why you do what you do. Unlike therapy (which I am a huge fan of, having logged plenty of my own couch time), coaching will help you take specific steps to move forward toward a new way of living. A therapist diagnoses and treats psychological problems, often looking at the past as a guide. It's very important and life changing work. As a matter of fact, I often work with clients who are simultaneously seeing a therapist – and it's great! These people are usually very open to change and make terrific progress.

And, guess what? People have successfully changed their lives without alienating their children or divorcing their spouse! People get balance in their lives without losing anything important – just by focusing on what's <u>really</u> important.

Knowing why you're doing what you're doing sounds so simple. But it requires honesty, openness and a willingness to change. You have to understand yourself so you can say no to that which keeps you stuck in a rut, and yes to that which brings you joy and allows you to grow.

What does it take to get out of your hectic and purposefully busy life? Again, it's simple.

It'll start when you say to yourself, "I can't go on like this anymore. This is not a fun, happy life" – that's when you know it's time to start making changes.

That, friends, is when you ask for help.

MIND YOUR OWN BUSINESS

IMAGINE YOU'RE A BUSINESS OWNER. SAY YOU HAVE A restaurant and you do a fair business, but you could always use more customers and revenue. One day a guy walks in and asks if you cater. You think a moment and say to yourself, "Well, food's food. I guess I can cater" and, voila! You've got a new line of business – you're a caterer.

Imagine another person comes in to the restaurant and says, "Charlie, you're a capable person and I like you a lot. Can I pay you to wallpaper my bathroom?"

Now, wait a second. Catering is to restaurant, as wallpapering is to…what?

This is exactly the moment many small business owners get off track. Especially when money's short. A client requests something that's not particularly in your sweet spot, but you do it, thinking, "Gotta get me some money." The end result: you spend less time on your business, it suffers and, voila! You have less money.

Saying no is hard. It's particularly hard to say no to earning money when you really need the cash. But think about it this way: saying no frees up your time to earn money building your business and doing more of what you like.

How do you know if what you're being offered is a new, lucrative business opportunity or just a waste of time? Glad you asked. Here are my Three Handy Things To Ask Yourself When Offered a Business Opportunity (catchy title, huh?):

What Do I Want For My Business? As a restaurateur, I want to offer good, well-prepared meals to people at fair prices. [Just as an aside, this is the quick and easy question anyone can ask themselves to come up with a mission statement – you just saved yourself thousands in consulting fees.]

Will This Opportunity Help Build My Business or Not? Catering allows the restaurateur to continue to offer good, well-prepared meals to people at fair prices. It's only the delivery system that changes. However, wallpapering doesn't allow the fulfillment of his mission statement in any way, shape or form.

How Do I Feel About This Opportunity? If you feel conflicted or uneasy or downright icky about it, use the Force, Luke, and listen to your feelings. If you feel uneasy before it even starts, imagine how you'll feel when six months go by and you're not cooking any meals – just endlessly wallpapering bathrooms.

And, you're saying to me, I don't own my own business. This is not relevant to me. Oh, really?

Most of us face moments when we are offered something that we could do but aren't sure if we should do. I'm suggesting that my Three Handy Things To Ask Yourself can be used whenever you need to evaluate doing something new.

What do I want for my life? Will this help me grow, or not? How do I feel about this?

Whenever you need to sort out options, and feel... oh, overwhelmed or uncertain or just plain icky, take the time to remember what it is you set out to do — <u>then,</u> feel free to say yes or no.

༄

In-Box Management

Like most folks, I have a couple of different email in-boxes. One's more for work, one's more for fun, and one seems to be the catchall for hundreds of spam messages. That's right, hundreds – every day.

I get messages for products – how do I put this delicately – to enhance the size and prowess of a particular body part that's not a standard equipment on the female form. From these messages, I have learned that this particular body part requires quite a lot tending, in terms of medication, creams, patches and powders. I had no idea. Always seemed rather straightforward to me: Stimulus. Response. Done.

Oh, and I get many touching messages from lonely young women who'd like to show me their pictures, dear things.

I had no idea that I had so many kinsmen who die in Africa, Latin America and China, leaving immense fortunes which can be mine if I cooperate with certain widowed wives of former dignitaries of said nations.

People write daily to sell me OEM software, whatever that is, and "genuine replica watches". Let's see, it's "genuine" and "replica" – sounds surprisingly like "fake".

The other day I received a message from the unfortunately named "Cosimo Kiang", who wanted to give me $500, just for clicking a button. Where do they manufacture these names, anyway? Throwing darts at a phone book?

Every couple of days, I scan through these messages looking for an authentic message from a real person asking me a real question. This trolling and culling takes too much of my time, and I always worry that I've overlooked or deleted something of real importance.

I hate spam. It sucks my time and attention and gets me all distracted and fidgety.

But you know what? The deluge of stupid, time-wasting, ridiculous messages is not restricted to my email in-box. Nope, I get plenty of spam addressed to one other mailbox I sort through regularly – the in-box between my ears.

You know these kinds of spam messages: Be thinner. Be younger. Be older. Be smoother. Be tougher. Be gentler. Be taller. Be sexier. Be buff. Be wealthy. Be #1. Be as self-sacrificing as Mother Teresa.

In short: Be something other than what you are.

The spam between my ears doesn't help me live my best possible life. It clogs me up, paralyzes me, helps me feel inadequate and unsuccessful. So, I've taken to sorting through and culling those messages, too. The good news is that I've finally arrived at the place where I receive the message, decide whether it's something to pay attention to or not, then click that old delete button.

So satisfying.

If you have a ton of spam in the in-box between your ears, maybe it's time to do a major purge. Better yet, set some filters so the most annoying, time consuming, distracting messages go to the trash before you ever see them!

The best messages are those that lift you up, reinforce the best part of you, remind you what makes you uniquely wonderful, prompt you to live authentically, and allow you to change that which holds you back.

The rest? A spam-like waste of time.

༄

Either/Or

"I CAN STAY IN MY JOB AND HAVE ENOUGH MONEY, OR I CAN DO what I love and be broke."

"I can't be happy as long as I'm married to Clyde."

"Since I have been a full-time parent for the last ten years, the only job I can possibly get won't pay very much."

All statements I have heard in the last month – that's true.

But they're not true statements. Sure, they feel true to the folks saying them, but they're really either/or, black/white statements. They're what's called "limiting beliefs". Either/or statements like this serve a great purpose – they keep us pretty well stuck.

Because... is it true that you have to be broke to do what you love? Hmmmn. Oprah looks like she loves what she does and she's doing all right. Bill Gates? He seems pretty happy. Steve Jobs is passionate about what he does, and he gets all the Istuff he can use. Bono gets to be a multi-millionaire rock star AND do good while wearing cool sunglasses.

Either/or statements serve as fear-based predictors of what's going to happen. If you go into a job interview with the mindset, "Since I've been a full-time parent for 10 years, I can't ask for too much" – guess what? You won't. Confidence in your own self-worth is reflected in that thought, and you telegraph it to everyone you meet. How much stronger to say, "Even though I've been out of the workforce for 10 years, I bring great skills and excellent contacts – I'm worth what they've budgeted for this position's salary."

Living in black/white, either/or land is one way to make sure you're always right. "I can't be happy if I'm married to Clyde" – a popular kind of statement. Saying this, you will discard any experience that might show that you could be happy, or, heaven forbid, that you actually like Clyde. You will pursue, or maybe even create, opportunities to be unhappy with Clyde. What if you turned it around and figured ways to see if you could be happy with Clyde, oh, like, let's see: counseling, mutual hobbies, actually talking to him…

Often when we "can't be happy" it's not because of someone else, but because of something within ourselves. And we owe it to the Clydes of the world to work on that before laying our own dissatisfaction at their feet.

Living in the gray between black/white is the challenge, and the gift. It's saying, "I can lose weight while eating fewer carbs." It's saying, "I may have to start the work I love on the side or as a volunteer, while I keep my job for the income." It's "I can be happy with or without Clyde – it's up to me."

There are "motivational speakers" out there who tout the idea "You CAN have it all." Which is, poppets, yet another black/white statement. The beauty of living in the gray is replacing "either/or" with "and". It's so much more balanced to believe, "I can have some of this and some of that," or, even more true, "I can have whatever I need."

Contrary to popular belief, life is not all or nothing. The key to getting unstuck is getting un-attached to the either/or thoughts that immobilize us, and recognizing them for the limiting beliefs they are.

In fashion, it's often said that this color or that color is the "new black". In life, the key to happiness is replacing black/white with the best of both – to live in the shades of gray that are truly flattering.

༄

THE ABSENCE OF PERFECT

I STRUGGLED WITH WRITING TODAY. I COULDN'T FIND THE perfect opening sentence – the one line that would grab you and compel you to read on. The perfectly turned phrase. An ideal piece of writing that you would remember forever, and forward to your friends and family with a tear in your eye and a lump in your throat. The Great American Blog.

I just couldn't get there. I had writer's block. I was stuck.

So, I asked myself one of my favorite questions, "In the absence of the perfect solution, what are my options?"

In the absence of the perfect intro, my options were a) to not write anything, b) to just write something c) to go shopping.

Just for the record, I chose b). As appealing as c) was. And I got unstuck.

When you're stuck in any aspect of your life, ask yourself the same question, "In the absence of the perfect solution, what are my options?"

Being stuck is tough. Going neither forward, nor back – just standing in place, watching the world whirl by. Removed. Stuck.

Pursuit of perfection often leads to stuck-ness. "I can't have guests until my house is perfect" or "I have to finish my MBA before I can apply for a new job" or "I guess I'm still single because I'm just too picky" – all statements in pursuit of perfection. All statements which keep us stuck.

Shooting for the ideal is what we're taught from the time we're dandled on grandma's knee. "Don't settle! Hold onto your dreams! You can be anything you want to be!" But the dark side to what your grandma told you is that sometimes holding on to the ideal prevents you from doing anything at all.

Which is safe. But stuck.

When I pursue perfection, I limit my vision to only that which corresponds to my narrow vision of "perfect". According to advertisers, the perfect solution for any single woman is a hunky, hairless, pouting, slightly sweating guy who stares vaguely into the distance. Were I to hold on to that ideal, I would miss the OK-looking, kind, thoughtful, intelligent, slightly hairy available guy who would be a good partner for me.

Perfection is elusive. It's a soap bubble of joy. It only exists when we're not blowing too hard. Perfection is in the spontaneous hug of a four year old. It's in the kindness of strangers. It's there in a great big belly laugh. It's in the last place you'd expect to find it.

Perfection ceases to exist the harder you look for it.

So, when holding out for the ideal prevents you from actually living your life, and keeps you stuck, know your options. Choose one that will enlarge your experience and allow you to grow.

When you do, you'll stop being stuck. It'll be perfect.

AUTHENTICALLY YOU

There was a time in my life when I said "yes" when I meant "no", and "no" when I meant "yes". Looking back, I realize I did it because that's what I thought people wanted from me. And I wanted to be the person folks wanted me to be.

I said "yes" so often that my friend Fran gave me a t-shirt which read "Stop Me Before I Volunteer Again" which I wore to the next PTA meeting. I happened to be the PTA President at the time. Excellent team building message, don't you think?

I said "yes" because saying "no" might have meant someone would be unhappy with me. It made no never mind if I was unhappy. My own need to be liked was more important than my need to be happy.

And I was not happy. Because I was not allowing myself to be authentically Michele. I was allowing others to determine who I might be. Power, power – who's got the power? It was anybody but me.

I just re-read a book I've learned so much from: *The Wizard of Oz and Other Narcissists* by Eleanor Payson. The approach Payson takes in this book – what living with, working with, or being raised by a narcissist does to a person's self-esteem, coping mechanisms and future relationships – is insightful. But I got something new from my recent re-read – the idea of self-reflection as an indicator of emotional and mental health.

People with a character disorder, such as narcissism, are incapable of self-reflection. I also think people who are sleepwalking through their lives often avoid self-reflection or self-observation because they are afraid of waking up and living fully. Maybe they are afraid of being authentically themselves.

I am here to tell you that self-reflection is the path to authentic living. When you know who you are, how you feel and what you like – not what others want you to be, feel or like – and you live it, that's authenticity, baby.

There's an index card on my computer monitor. On it are scratched three simple questions. For me, they are the heart of my own self-reflection.

- Why have I drawn this experience to me at this time?

- What is this experience trying to teach me?

- How can I use this situation to help me be a better person?

I refer to this card so often that these three questions have become my intuitive framework, especially when I am tempted to say "yes" when I really want to say "no". The opportunity to say "no", and mean it, often comes to me when I need to remember to keep my boundaries intact. Sometimes, it comes as a chance to help maintain my priorities – and not take responsibility for executing yours. I've learned that when I focus on executing other people's priorities, it's frequently at the expense of my own.

Every single time I say "no" when I want to say "no", I reinforce that I am a Self worth being. All by myself. Regardless of whether you like me and my answer to your request, or not. When I stand up for myself, I am standing for my own authentic Me. That is a shift from my old way of being, and it feels really good. It feels like I am expressing my true self.

And, boy howdy, I become a better person when I only say "yes" when I mean "yes". I do a better job. I'm not overcommitted. I'm more focused. I say "yes" because I really and truly want to do what's asked of me. Believe me, if I say "yes", you are going to see and feel my passion.

Being authentically me means that I honor my choices, and I honor my abilities. I'm living my passions. I'm feeling all my feelings. And expressing them. And when I'm authentically me, I make space for you to be authentically you. How? Because it's perfectly OK with me if you are mad, happy, sad, silly, loving, offbeat, generous, hurt, wacky or meditative. Because I'm all those things, too.

Supply & Demand

"I DON'T EVEN KNOW WHO I AM ANY MORE," THE 40-SOMETHING woman across the table said to me. "Am I just someone's mom? Someone's wife? The chauffeur? The person who does the laundry and cooks the meals? Is that all I am?"

It's a perverse irony – we love to do things for others, yet by doing so we often lose ourselves. We're always ready to help others, always available to tend to that which needs tending. We're so accommodating that our help becomes expected rather than appreciated.

It's a fact that when things become too easy, too plentiful, too ubiquitous, they are often taken for granted. This is true whether it's a person, place or thing. The bottom line is that when something is too available, it is less valuable.

But that's supply and demand for you. Too much supply in the system yields lower value. More demand than supply raises value.

If you are someone who derives meaning and purpose from being needed, you may find that your willingness to drop your priorities to help others meet their priorities devalues both you and what you want to do.

Here's an example: The laundry is always done on time. Your family comes to expect it. There is always food, and no one fixes meals but you. You help with homework. You come running when called. Even when you are knee deep in paying bills, figuring income taxes or coordinating the big fundraiser, you drop what you are doing to help someone else. You feel frustrated because you never seem to finish anything, and you can't concentrate long enough to focus on the big picture.

Another example: You have a big project on your dance card. You chunk it up into doable steps and make a plan for getting it all done on time. Then Jim pops his head into your cube and says, "Can you help me with the Framastan contract?" You like being needed, especially by Jim (who is a good guy but REALLY needy), so you say, "Sure!" Next thing you know, Jim is presenting and not mentioning that you helped in any way – and your own project is still not done.

An example of putting your own needs last: Your source of soul-boosting strength is full sweat mountain biking. However, whenever you go biking you feel guilty if you don't bring your two year old along in a bike seat, and your five year old along on his own bike. They can't manage trails, so you stick to the flat path. You never break a sweat and your soul is teased, but not nourished.

When your needs are always trumped by another's needs, you telegraph the message "I am not important." Oh, you may feel important in the doing, and in being needed. But if your own objectives and priorities are not valued – even by you – your own objectives and priorities will fall by the wayside.

When you provide endless supply, the value of what you provide is diminished. In fact, your very sense of self becomes diminished.

How do you get supply and demand into appropriate balance? Start by honoring your own needs, values, objectives and priorities. Easier said than done? OK, I'll give you a script.

Your child yells, "Hey, come look at this!" You say, "Sweetie pie, I am working on the taxes and can't come right now. Can you explain to me what you see?" That way, if what he wants you to see is a commercial for Snappy-Poppy O's or an escaped gerbil or, oh, blood, you can react accordingly. You are also teaching him that what you do is important and deserves respect. A great life lesson.

Jim asks for help on the Framastan contract. You say, "Jim, I'd love to help you but I have to get this project done by Thursday at 3pm. Can I help you after that?" In all likelihood, Jim will move on and look for another sucker to do his work for him. And you have proven that you are not that sucker.

You plan to go mountain biking to work up a sweat and feed your soul. Keep that objective in mind and leave the kids at home in the care of someone wonderful (then, when you get home and are showered, push that caring someone out the door for his or her own soul-feeding time). Prioritize your "me time" – because doing so helps you be a better parent.

Sometimes your over-supply of "help and assistance" can be read as "You are not capable of doing this for yourself" or "You will make a muddle of this, so I am going to take care of it." Both of these sentiments completely disempower the other person. Think about it: when you go on a girl's weekend once a year and always arrange a babysitter to support your husband, what message are you sending? That he's incapable of effective parenting? Then why in the world do you complain that he never does anything? You've already sent him the message that he can't, loud and clear.

We lose ourselves, like the 40-year old woman I talked with, when we devalue our selves by being too available, and not honoring our own needs and objectives. So, be careful of what you supply. Calibrate your help and assistance to meet reasonable demands. Keep your value up by giving others the chance to meet their own demands. You have a right to know who you are, and you get it through a steady supply of self-respect.

I Am, I Said

It's nice to have friends. It's especially nice to have friends like Lauri and Anne – the kind of friends who drop by for tea and bring great ideas. Oh, and cookies. We cannot overlook the importance of cookies.

We sat the other day, sipping, munching thoughtfully, until Anne piped up with: "OK, so we were talking about something in the car on the way over and wanted to hear what you think."

I was actually thinking that the cookies were really good. But I'm often able to stretch my brain just a bit. "Uhmrrgh," I responded, through cookie crumbles, which means, "Bring it on."

"Ever notice how often we say 'I'm not' and how infrequently we say 'I am'?" Anne asked.

I was struck speechless by the simplicity of Anne's point.

Boy, we spend so much time thinking about what we're not.

Coming from "I'm not" is coming from a lack, or a deficit. "I'm not" means not enough – not tall enough, not thin enough, not young enough, not rich enough, not smart enough, not anything enough.

"I'm not" keeps us in a continual state of stress, feeling like we haven't/can't/won't get it all done. And we won't. Because we're not enough.

But if we could shift all those "I'm nots" to "I ams"... think of the difference. Owning your own strengths. Standing in your own power. Relying on what you've got, rather than what you haven't.

"I am"... good at taking care of my aging parents. "I am" ... a good mentor. "I am" ... a good friend. "I am" ... alive.

Recently I taught a teleclass to a group of students and heard myself saying, "I'm pretty good at networking." And I caught myself, internally, doing a self-check: was I bragging? Didn't Mama say, "Don't get too big for your britches. You're no better than anyone else?"

She sure did. But it didn't feel like bragging. It felt like truth. And, guess what? It is.

Make a list of your "I ams". Own your "I ams". Treasure them. They're your truths. They're what makes you, you.

And every time you find yourself stuck in "I'm not", turn it around and say a quick "I am". Such as, "OK, I'm not a 25 year old supermodel with more money than sense and no responsibilities, but I am..."

Go ahead – fill in your own blank.

The Company You Keep

My first job after college was working for a beer company. Yep, I was hired to take on the onerous duty of selling beer to college students. Such hard work! For undertaking this major, heavy-lifting responsibility, I got a company car, an expense account, tickets to major sporting events all over the Pacific Northwest and all the gimme t-shirts a girl could want.

Nice work if you can get it, believe me.

At the time, and probably even today, the beer industry was dominated by men. I can't tell you how many times I was the only woman in the room. It was a guy business, run by guys, governed by guy rules – and I sure learned to play by guy rules.

Which meant I swore like a sailor.

Everywhere I went – every warehouse, every meeting, every bar, every grocery store – people were using swear words. They were used as adjectives. As nouns. As verbs. Even as dangling participles.

I swam in an ocean of obscenity. And I took to it like a fish to water.

Imagine my surprise when, in my next job, I let go a stream of what I considered normal, creative invective and the room fell deadly quiet. Guess what? My new colleagues didn't swear. I felt like a fish out of water. A fish with a potty mouth.

Group dynamics certainly govern our behavior. What's acceptable to one crowd may be completely unacceptable to another. The trick is to find a group which supports that which is best in us – rather than a group that appeals to, how shall I say it? Our baser instincts.

There's a public service announcement on TV now which shows a stick figure lounging in a window, smoking a joint. He offers a hit to the dog. The dog declines the opportunity. The stick figure says, "I feel bad about what I'm doing. If you did it with me, I'd feel less bad." Maybe the dog's name is B-I-N-G-O, because that's what I felt like saying when I saw the ad. Bingo! People who feel bad about what they are doing need me to do it, too, so they can feel less bad.

In her book *Not Just Friends*, Dr. Shirley Glass suggests that one of the ways to affair-proof your marriage is to associate with people who are not only friends of marriage in general, but friends of your marriage in particular. In fact, Dr. Glass' research shows that associating with people who are in affairs, or who condone, support or encourage affairs, increases the likelihood that your marriage will end in divorce.

It's like a new norm is invented by the company you keep. If everyone swears, then it's normal to swear. If everyone takes office supplies home, then it's not stealing – it's actually OK to put that Xerox copier in your pocketbook and haul it home. If people are rewarded for swindling clients, then clients get swindled. If everyone is cheating on their spouse, then it's not cheating, really – it's fun, it's cool, it's how the game is played. It may be unethical, but it's the norm. And when you live unethically, day in and day out, your self-esteem erodes.

That's why finding your "tribe" of like-minded friends is vitally important to your marriage, to your workplace, to your happiness – to your sense of self.

Friends help you be your best self. They support your personal growth, are objective and appropriately affirming. I say "appropriately" because it would be perfectly fine with me if a friend were less than affirming – especially if I had wandered off on some weird track that was not really that good for me. Like if I were spending day after day in my jammies eating junk food, not bathing, muttering to myself and watching back-to-back Rachel Ray shows. Some people call that "bad". Other people call it "March, 2004."

Moving on.

Henri Nouwen, one of my favorite spiritual writers, defined love as making a safe place for another person to be fully themselves. My kids' pediatrician has a framed print on his wall, "Let him be left-handed if that's how he's made." Love, then, is letting someone be left-handed. Or gassy. Or opinionated. Or a Rachel Ray fan.

But being a friend also means you have the obligation to raise the impact of their negative or destructive behaviors with them.

The moment to evaluate a friendship is when, in the process of your friend fully being themselves, you find that you cannot be fully yourself. If their full expression is hurtful, dangerous or negative to you, you have every right to say something and to lovingly detach – to give them a ton of safe space to be themselves.

Alcoholics often find that they need new friends after sobriety, because many of their old friends consciously or subconsciously promote drinking. That's one reason why recovering alcoholics get sponsors – the sponsor is the beginning of a new social network, one which supports healthy, affirming activities, yet is lovingly supportive when the person in recovery slips back into hurtful habits. The sponsor creates a positive space for the alcoholic to be fully himself.

Toxic friendships are often based on being in a negative space together. How do you know if you're in one? If you feel used, you're probably being used. If you feel demeaned and belittled, then you're not in a situation which helps you grow. If you feel you can't be fully yourself with your friends, then you definitely haven't found your tribe. Relationships like this are not about growth or overcoming or affirmation. Rather, these friendships serve to keep all participants down, so nothing and no one has to change. They exist so other people won't feel so bad.

When eyes open and one person begins to grow, however, these friendships end because what they're built on is not solid. And that's OK. Because when you're out of a bad situation, you have the chance to find a good one.

Look at your friendships. Do they support you? Do they affirm you? Do they reflect your values, your ethics, your best self? If they do, then congratulations.

You've found your tribe.

NEED MORE TIME?

NEED MORE TIME? HAVE ENOUGH TIME TO GET EVERYTHING done? Are there things that remain on your to-do list – for years? Stuff you never get around to tackling, oh, like exercising, finding a new job or actually having friends?

It's a modern predicament many of us face. But here's a strategy that really works: simply think about your time differently.

Imagine you have 100 units of energy to spend each day. You can't take from yesterday, because those 100 units are gone. You can't borrow from tomorrow, because those units belong to tomorrow.

You've just got 100 to use today. How will you allocate them?

First, you have to assess how you're spending your time. Take a pen and paper (or a crayon and the back of an envelope, or a Sharpie and a docile housepet) and write down everything you did yesterday. Start with what time you woke up, when you got out of bed, what you did next, and next, and next – all the way to the time you went to sleep.

Now, remember: how you use your time reveals your true priorities. How did you use your time yesterday? What does that reveal about your priorities?

Let's say you have a priority to find a new job, but allocated no energy to that pursuit yesterday (or the day before, or the day before). Could it be that you really don't want a new job – but that your spouse is pressuring you to make more money? Or, your daddy said you'd be successful when you made regional manager, but you'd rather not do sales at all?

When you really want something, you'll allocate energy to it. Plain and simple.

Friends, it is also possible to use "lack of time" as a way to avoid taking action, or to avoid something unpleasant. If you think that's the case, look at the priority you allegedly want to pursue. Do you really want it? Are you avoiding something? Is the priority yours? Or someone else's?

A priority that someone else places upon you is called a "should" – such as: you should always put ketchup in a dish, not serve it in the bottle at dinner time; you should be a doctor and make a ton of money; you should have a housekeeper; you shouldn't have a housekeeper; you should keep your house tidy at all times; you should be thinner, smarter, hotter or blonder.

When really all you should be is – you. Shoulds limit us. They force us to serve another person's priorities rather than our own. We depart from who we are in an effort to meet someone else's needs – which may not allow us to be our best. That, my friends, is the path to unhappiness. Let's all focus on being happy, and eliminate shoulds. Agreed?

If you look at how you spent your 100 units of energy yesterday and realize that another person took 70 units, they better have a darn good reason. Most of us are ready to help another person in crisis – but when that crisis goes on for weeks, months, years, you need to take a hard look and ask yourself whether the energy suck is keeping you from reaching your own priorities. If so, set some boundaries and re-shift your energy units to serve you better.

You have 100 units of energy to spend today. How will you use them to support <u>your</u> priorities?

Life's Little Aggravations

A LOVELY MAN OF MY ACQUAINTANCE RANG ME UP THIS WEEK and told me he enjoys what I write. I demurely blushed. Then, being the genial problem-solver extraordinaire that he is, he added: "Could you write something about living with day-to-day problems? Not everyone, you know, has problems in the workplace."

No, it's true that not everyone has problems in the workplace. Plenty of my gazillion-and-twelve readers don't even have a workplace! But nearly everyone is vexed by daily frustrations that add up to make them feel stressed and overwhelmed.

You know what I mean: The fellow at the baseball game who's drunk, spills everything and screams obscenities in front of your kindergartner. Your upstairs neighbor who seems to walk the floor in golf spikes every morning at 2am. The gal yakking on her cell phone while the traffic behind her piles up because she's not taking the right turn on red. The woman in the express checkout with a full basket, who, at the last minute, can't locate her checkbook or pen.

How, indeed, can one deal with those issues in a positive and purposeful way?

Ah, now we're getting to Michele's Big Vision Of Life. Prepare yourself – there are several tenets we'll have to cover.

First, you can never know what's going on in another person's head unless they tell you. The woman in front of you in the checkout line may live alone with 56 cats, and that trip to the store may be her only interaction with another human being in the whole week. Her momentary connection with the clerk, and you, may mean more to her than you can ever know. The gal on the cell phone? She might be a doctor racing to the hospital, making sure the emergency orders she's issuing are absolutely understood by the oncology nurse on the other end of the line.

Since you can't know what's in another person's mind, you have two choices: decide they're purposefully making your life difficult, or, they're doing the best they can.

Guess which choice helps you feel more peaceful.

Second, people don't have to be exactly like you to be right. You may go to the store to get milk and eggs, but other people go there to get connection and affirmation. A little tolerance and acceptance of different motivations and expectations can go a long way toward reducing your frustration.

Folks are frustrated that other people aren't exactly like themselves in plenty of situations. I know churches where people are frustrated because not everyone in the congregation approaches worship the same way. I know offices where people are angry because not everyone is a driven Type-A who's wedded to his job. I know marriages in which both partners futilely endeavor to mold each other into their own shape. Each of these situations overlooks the big point – we're all different, and vive la difference! Different outlooks, experiences and expectations bring richness and fullness to life. It certainly feels like I'm powerful and in control when I think "it would be better if everyone were just like me!", but what that really is... is fear. It's the fear of that which challenges my comfort zone.

Third, you can operate out of fear or you can operate out of love. When you operate out of fear, you limit your world view to that which cannot hurt you. Fear doesn't allow you to question your own beliefs, or analyze your own mistakes, or even consider that someone else might have a valid point. Fear is a closed, keep-myself-safe approach. Fear is "if he really knew what I was like inside, he'd leave me, so I'm going to keep my true Self hidden and hope for the best." That particular fear leads to a horrible death – the death of the sense of who you really are and of what's important to you. It's the death of true authenticity.

Love, on the other hand, is transparent, authentic and open. Love is all those things we've read – patient and kind, understanding and tolerant, hopes all things and endures all things. Love truly covers all transgressions. Henri Nouwen, one of my favorite writers, said that love exists when I create a safe place for another person to be fully himself. Even if when they're being fully themselves they tick me off. Between you and me, that's when I lovingly give them a whole lotta space to be fully themselves.

Because coming from love does not mean you abandon your boundaries or forget your limits. No, keeping those intact help keep you intact. Coming from love doesn't mean you're a doormat, either. Coming from love simply means living life with freedom from fear.

When daily life vexes you, you have a choice. You can come from a place of fear, with the expectation that you're going to be hurt, or you can come from a place of love, and the expectation that, although you can't know what motivates another person, you can be charitable, kind and open to learning something new from them. And about yourself.

If we could all shift away from fear and toward love, our collective vexation would diminish. Wouldn't that be something? It would be as if the entire world stepped back, took a giant exhale and relaxed.

And that would be Michele's Big Vision Of Life.

∽

The Way of Transition

THE SEASONS ARE CHANGING. I CAN SEE IT OUTSIDE MY window. There are little buds on the Japanese maple. Tulip tips are pushing up through the ground. There's a light, warm quality to the breeze – it's bringing spring.

I love spring. Since I can remember, spring has meant happiness. Sure, it's my birthday in a few weeks and the kid in me loves that. But the soon-to-be 47 year old grown-up in me has a different reason for joy.

I give a class on Managing Transition. Did you know that each transition begins with an ending? Odd, but so. We end a job, or a relationship, or an old way of being. Then we enter what writer William Bridges calls The Neutral Zone. I like to think of it as the Gray Period.

In my class, I liken the Gray Period to winter. Trees look dead. Grass looks dead. It's cold. People hunker down. There's a certain bleak stillness to winter. But inside those lifeless looking trees and plants, plenty is going on. Within each dormant tree are the tiny little beginnings of buds waiting to burst forth.

And so it is, too, with people in transition. They endure an ending which may bring grief, change, uncertainty, immobilization. Then they hunker down in a bleak stillness, seemingly doing nothing… but inside, if they could peek, so much is growing, changing and shifting. Inside, there's a new beginning.

The new beginning is as inevitable as Spring. A renewal. A new start. A new optimism.

When people in transition tell me there's no hope, I usually challenge them. Saying there's no hope is like telling me there's no Spring! Honey, just as sure as having a birthday, there's always a Spring.

Certainly, March can come in like a lion or a lamb – it's an unpredictable month. And transition is equally unpredictable. One can never know the look and shape of a new beginning, nor can we know how it will impact our lives. And perhaps that's what people who voice "no hope" are trying to address. It's not that there's no hope – it's just that there's no control.

Control is such an overrated thing. I have a book on my desk (which I've not yet read), called *A Perfect Mess* by Eric Abrahamson and David Freedman which posits that disorder can spark creativity. On the book jacket (which I have read), it says, "Though it flies in the face of almost universally accepted wisdom, moderately disorganized people, institutions, and systems frequently turn out to be more efficient, more resilient, more creative, and in general more effective than highly organized ones…"

In my work I've found that those who approach the Gray Period with a certain level of uncertainty, disorder and, most importantly, openness, have a better opportunity to find a novel or creative approach which often sparks their new beginning.

On an episode of The Simpsons, Homer was, once again, out of a job. His daughter Lisa was going through the want ads, looking for a job for her dad. "Dad, here's one," she said. "Wanted: a technical supervisor." "Oh, Lisa," Homer whined. "I could never do that job. I'm not a technical supervisor, I'm a supervising technician!"

The Gray Period is a time for seeing connections – to see how a technical supervisor can become a supervising technician. How an at-home mom can become a business owner. How a lawyer can become a non-profit executive. How an engineer can become a clergywoman. How a suddenly motherless woman can learn to nurture herself. How down-sizing, or divorce, or even death, can be the best thing that ever happened to you.

And that's where I find joy. I utterly embrace transition in all its messy splendor. I welcome it for the hope it engenders in me. Because I know that for every ending, there is a new beginning. Every. Single. Time. It may not feel possible in the middle of your own personal Gray Period, but, believe me, Spring is there – just waiting to burst forth.

How will you know when your Gray Period has ended? My friend, when you feel the warm breeze blowing across your face, and see the trees bud, and tulip tops poking up, you will know. You have a new start. You have Spring. Even if your new beginning comes in a month other than March.

༄

When Times Are Tough

It's been a tough couple of weeks for yours truly. I've faced a 3-D crisis: Death, Disease and Disappointment. A long-time friend died; a woman dear to me is ill; one of my readers has been given a scary diagnosis; and, someone didn't do what he said he had done. All in all, a challenging time.

How do we get through crisis? How do we function when times are tough? How can we make the best of a bad situation?

Here are some tactics you can use when you face tough times:

First, don't hurry through difficulties. I know, I know. Sounds counter-intuitive, huh? But finding a solution to a set of difficult problems may take time — and if you rush, you can find yourself applying the wrong solutions, which can completely compound the problem.

Second, accept the gifts difficulty has to offer. Another counter-intuitive thought? Not really. It's only by fully experiencing the lows that we can fully experience the highs. I believe it's impossible to live in bliss. Bliss is something that can be touched and savored in the moment — but it's incredibly hard to sustain. Fully feeling sadness, hurt, vulnerability, disappointment and fear allows us to understand and learn. And to remember we're only human.

Third, make sure you are surrounded by a team of people ready to help and support you. In my case, my team "floats" depending on what I need. Sometimes my team includes a lawyer (or two), an accountant, a teacher, a consultant or another coach. Sometimes my team consists of three wise women and two bottles of wine. The latter is infinitely more fun than the former, with no offense meant to lawyers and accountants who can be fun in their own special ways. In my "Thinking About Starting Your Own Business" and "Writing Your Own Personal Strategic Plan" workshops, I ask participants to inventory the folks they'll need on their team to meet their objectives. It's a good idea to identify your "crisis team" when times are good — so when times get tough, you know who to call. And, if you don't know who to call, rely on friends, family and colleagues to give you good referrals.

Fourth, if your crisis takes you by complete surprise and you have that deer-in-the-headlights feeling — do this: think of someone you know who's experienced your crisis before and pretend you're her. "Carol would ask these questions," you can tell yourself. Then proceed to ask all of Carol's questions, which may prompt a few of your own. Our friends the mental health professionals call this "modeling" but you can also call it "surviving" — just until you have the information and strength to get going again.

Finally, remind yourself that you are a resilient person. You haven't gotten this far without weathering a few storms, right? Reflect on other tough times you have faced–you made it through, didn't you? You learned something. You made deeper connections with others. You grew stronger.

When times are tough, we are being challenged to our very core to dig deep and be the best people we can be in that moment. The good news is that tough times don't last forever. And when they pass, our hearts are open to grateful living – and anticipation of the inevitable good times to come.

༄

Risky Business

BACK IN THE SUMMER OF 1972, "STUCK IN THE MIDDLE WITH You" was a hit for a band called Stealers Wheel — the song was written by bandmates Gerry Rafferty and Joe Egan. Know the lyrics?

"Well I don't know why I came here tonight
I got the feeling that something ain't right
I'm so scared in case I'll fall off my chair
And I'm wondering how I'll get down the stairs
Clowns to the left of me, jokers to the right, here I am
Stuck in the middle with you

"Yes I'm stuck in the middle with you
And I'm wondering what it is I should do
It's so hard to keep this smile from my face
Losing control yeah, I'm all over the place
Clowns to the left of me, jokers to the right, here I am
Stuck in the middle with you."

It's no fun being stuck between clowns and jokers. Feels like whatever way you go, you'll lose. Nothing will ever change.

Net effect? You stay on your chair, trying desperately not to fall off.

When you're stuck – stuck like Krazy Glue, or in a rut that's so deep you can't see a way out – you could take a stab at writing a hit song... or, you could just try something else.

That's my advice. That's all. Just try something else. Something risky.

Risk, I've found, is the best way to overcome being stuck. Taking a small risk every day moves you, perhaps ever so slightly away from your fear and toward happiness. Taking a small risk every day inches your comfort zone out just a tad. Before you know it, you're no longer stuck – you're out and moving, and have left the clowns and jokers behind.

I often suggest people go up to that which troubles them the most and shake that fear's hand. Often, the fear's not so big, bad and scary when you look it in the eye. Let's say your biggest stuck area is at work. You feel you can't say what needs to be said, that you are not respected and are taken for granted. Sound familiar?

So you need to get heard and have your voice respected. Big goal. Let's break it down into smaller bits...OK, for you, a teeny tiny risk might be to make a point at a meeting. Just one. You don't have to execute a coup d'etat, or monopolize, or bust heads. Just take a teeny tiny risk by speaking up instead of sitting and seething, and begin to claim your power.

Granted, ideas about what a risk is may differ widely. Volunteering to honcho a project at work may seem a huge risk to the introvert. A woman who does so much for others could find her risk in buying herself something nice. A man who worries that the life has gone out of his marriage may take a risk when he tells his wife he loves and admires her and wants the marriage to work. The widow makes her risk when she picks up the phone and connects with a friend.

How do you know if it's a risk? If it feels like a risk, it probably is. For me, risk feels like a little frisson of anxiety that bubbles in my belly, mixed with a tiny closure of the throat. But that's just me...

When I feel that feeling I know I'm facing a challenge – and I try to push myself to address it. At least part of it. Remember, risk is about enlarging your comfort zone so you can grow and become fuller and more happy. Risk is not about hurting yourself or others. Taking a little risk every day is a discipline that pays off when you look at your life and realize, hey, there's nothing holding me back. I'm not afraid! I'm not stuck in the middle! The only folks still stuck there are the jokers and the clowns.

༺༻

Cleaning a Closet

I cleaned out a closet the other day. "Yes," you're saying to yourself, "she lives such a glamorous life." So true.

I cleaned out a walk-in closet in preparation for a much needed paint job. It's been nine years since the closet was empty, let alone painted. It's past time for a thorough overhaul.

As I toted yet another armful of hanging clothes out, it occurred to me that I have way too much stuff. I was carrying junk I don't wear and don't even like too much, and I was carrying too much of it. And it wasn't just clothes. What were my high school yearbooks doing in there? Baby toys? (My kids are teens.) Two dozen books, a broken video camera, three shoeboxes full of photos, and assorted suitcases? In my clothes closet?

As I plopped the detritus of the closet into its Temporary Storage Area, I decided that the only things going back in the closet are things I really want in there.

Things I use.

Things I like.

Things that make me feel happy.

Thank goodness for paint jobs. Without this upcoming one, I wouldn't have taken the time to take a hard look at my stuff, dust the shelves and give the corners a good vacuuming.

Then it hit me: there's plenty of stuff to clean out of other closets. Like the closet between my ears. There's plenty of junk in there that's outdated, that I don't like, and that doesn't make me particularly happy.

How about you? Is now the time to get rid of the excess stuff you've accumulated – to streamline your life and your thoughts so you can be your best self?

Maybe you have an outdated idea about yourself – and it's holding you back. I worked with a woman recently who views herself as a struggling young homemaker, although her home is paid off, there is money in the bank and her kids are ready to go to college. Seeing herself as struggling feels comfortable, controllable and somehow appropriate. It's the way she's defined herself. It's her comfort zone. Not a happy comfort zone, but a comfort zone nonetheless.

She needs to clean out that closet.

Whether you're literally or figuratively ready to clean out a closet, now's the time. Examine everything that comes out of your closet – does it fit? Is it in good shape? Does it bring out the best in you? Do you like it? If your answer is "yes", keep it. If the answer is "no", give it away.

Letting go of that which holds us back or weighs us down, allows space to open for us to grow and start something new. It's time to clean closets.

The Difference Between Men and Women

Isn't the internet a wonderful thing? You can read something interesting, then click to something else quite interesting, which leads, hours later, to an utterly random yet extremely fascinating article, completely unrelated to what got you started.

Using just this circuitous method, I stumbled on an interview with researcher Beverly Whipple, recently named one of the world's 50 most influential living scientists by New Scientist magazine. Whipple, professor emeritus at Rutgers University, began her career as a nurse and switched to sex research 44 years ago when a patient asked if a man who had suffered a heart attack could ever have sex again. In the course of her career, she has answered that question and many others.

One line from the interview really jumped out at me. When asked the difference between men and women in terms of sex, Whipple replied, "Men are goal oriented, and women are pleasure oriented."

Well, now. That makes a ton of sense, doesn't it?

Then I wondered if there were other areas of life where this is true. Sure, some men are keen to experience, not just rush to a goal. And women are known to set and meet goals. But in the aggregate, the idea that men have one definition of success and women have another has implications in the boardroom, as well as the bedroom. As I pondered, I realized there are plenty of examples of this, especially if you exchange the word "pleasure" for "experience".

Think about shopping. A man goes into a Shopping Situation with a seek-and-destroy mindset: "I need two new shirts, a tie and boxers, then I'm out of here!" Women may have things they need to pick up, but also look at the possibilities. "Sharon would like this!" or "This might work for Tom." Women often shop with a friend, and make a day of it. They pay attention to ambiance, texture, sounds.

He has a goal. She's after an experience.

Another example? The NCAA Final Four bracket chart. Can you think of another more goal-oriented deal than that? A guy will completely fill in the bracket and track the progress of the teams to the ultimate goal – the #1 position. On the other hand, when I watch college basketball I am fascinated by the stories, "Brent, the power forward, Lucas Jones, certainly has faced adversity. He was raised by his loving, asthmatic grandmother in Waukegon's gritty inner city after he tragically lost his parents to a freak Zamboni incident at age 8. He's a mentor to little kids at the Girls and Boys Club, a ventriloquist and a straight A student." Ahhwww. Women are suckers for that stuff. It's all part of the experience.

Women are color commentators, men are play-by-play.

So, where else does it matter that men are goal oriented and women are experience oriented? Let's get back to sex. Many men, and plenty of women, feel that orgasm is the goal of sex. Some men feel that there must be "something wrong" if their partner doesn't climax. Yet, I was surprised to learn from Professor Whipple that over 70% of women report they do not have orgasm every time they have intercourse. Sadly, there are a lot of women, and men, who feel "less than" sexually when, in fact, they are quite normal. The average woman takes 20 minutes to become sexually aroused — and, how shall I say it, in the rush to make their goal, many men forget not only the time, but the day of the week [insert laugh track here].

Imagine the mutual satisfaction if a man was aware that the experience is what is important to a woman, rather than rating "success" on whether she did or didn't have an orgasm. What if he fully supported her "pleasure for the sake of pleasure" and de-emphasized orgasm? With less pressure to perform for both parties, there would be better, and dare I say it, <u>more</u> sex.

I have to write a word about "male performance". What a doofy phrase. As if the man performs and the woman applauds. As we've seen above, that's not always true. Take it from me, it's not a performance, gents. Writer Gary Zukav talks very eloquently about the power of the sexual connection in his book *The Seat of The Soul*. In that book, Zukav suggests that forgetting the spiritual aspect of sex strips it of its meaning. In that way, too, the idea of "male performance" strips sex of the mutuality of the moment.

Just understanding that he needs a goal and she needs an experience could transform a relationship. Rather than expecting him to love shopping, just like she does, a woman could say, "I am going to respect his need to seek-and-destroy when he's shopping and not browbeat him to enjoy it as much as I do." Or a man might plan an outing with a woman and say, "Rather than try to climb to the top of Mt. Baldy as fast as possible, I'm going to make sure Susan really enjoys the experience. We'll move at a reasonable pace and stop halfway to have a picnic lunch."

Wouldn't it be great if a male manager could acknowledge that there is more to work than meeting and beating objectives – and reward women who focus on team-building and systems strengthening? And a woman manager could recognize that the guys on the team need the satisfaction of having something to strive toward, and create a process to measure and reward progress toward the goal?

There is so much to learn and appreciate from the differences between men and women. If a man can learn from a woman to slow down and enjoy the experience, while the woman learns the satisfaction of making and reaching goals, a kind of relational balance can be had – a balance which makes life for each of them that much more full.

A Peaceful, Easy Feeling

One of the biggest challenges many of my coaching clients face is making a decision. It's as if choosing one course forever closes out all other options. "What if I hate it?" they ask. "What if I make the wrong choice?" And they stay stuck in the limbo land of indecision.

Let's get this on the table: there are indeed wrong choices, from a moral perspective. But some decisions have no moral component – in those cases there are only choices with differing consequences. We get wrapped around the axle when we think that our decisions are set in concrete, when, really, only a few of them are.

Choosing a college for your child – does it need to be The Perfect School? Not really. I've known plenty of successful people who transferred schools and ended up with pretty darn happy lives. Does it have to be The Perfect Job? Nope. I'll bet you know someone who actually left a job and found a better one. The Perfect Marketing Campaign? With modern tracking technologies, strategies can shift instantaneously. The Perfect Couch? Who among us has only one couch for their entire life?

Very few decisions are forever. Knowing that can be liberating. And should make your decision-making a tad easier.

So, here's my method for sorting through your many opportunities and fixing on the one with the best possible consequences — Consider It, Feel It, Do It.

Consider It: I suggest people get into a quiet place with no distractions. This immediately conjures up the lotus position for some people and their hands start to get all sweaty. It's hard to concentrate when water is pooling in your palms, don't you think? A quiet place for some people can be found in a brisk walk, driving, or repetitive physical activity – so find the way that works for you. When you get still, review your options. Pretend you have decided on one choice. What are the consequences of making that choice? What might happen? What do you get? What do you give up? As you weigh this choice, ask yourself, "If I do this, will I be in my integrity? Does this choice support my values?" If your value is to spend more time with your spouse and children, taking a job which requires 60 hours on the road every week is not going to get you more of what you want. It's actually going to get you less. It's at this point that you have to ask yourself, "Is it true that I want to spend more time with my spouse and kids?" Whatever the response, make sure it's really speaking to your truth and integrity – not what other folks think your values and integrity *should* be. When we make choices in conflict with our real integrity and values, we create tension and friction in our lives.

Feel It: Still holding the idea that you have made a choice, how does it feel in your body? In your heart? In your head? Your feelings matter, so pay attention. If you feel tension in your neck and shoulders or a big honking knot in the pit of your stomach as you consider your course, that's a big tip off that it may be the wrong direction for you to take at this time.

Of course, you also have to be honest with yourself. You can talk yourself into that 60 hour a week road warrior job because the money and benefits are great, but your body will find a way to tell you that your choice is against something you value – you'll get sick, you'll get depressed, you'll get all snippy – and you'll know you have to make another choice.

Do It: Here's the point where you decide. I call this "Opening The Chute" – as if you're a rodeo rider on the back of a bucking bronco. You can only mess with the rope in your hand and adjust your hat so much. At some point, you have to open the chute and take the ride. But here's the twist: you make your choice with a bit of detachment. That's right, it's just a test. While you're doing whatever you've chosen, you are testing to see if it's right. You refine your approach. You collect data about what you're doing. You keep feeling it in your body. You persist through "decider's remorse" and keep testing. If at some point your choice no longer feels right, stop. That's right. Just stop. And consider the new options that present themselves. That may mean a new job, it may mean a new school, it may mean a new marketing campaign or a new couch. And that's perfectly OK. It's simply another chance to test your decision-making skills.

Are you one of those people who equate difficulty with working hard? That is, "anything worth doing is going to be a chore?" If so, it will be a challenge for you to make a valid assessment of your tests, because you may have internalized the idea that adversity as a good thing. You may never have known the ease that comes from thoughtful decision-making. I can assure you it's out there, and once you experience it you'll never want to go back to banging your head against the wall.

When you go through the process I've outlined with each opportunity available to you, you will be able to sort through them and find the one with the most peaceful, easy feeling. That peaceful, easy feeling comes when you're in The Zone, when you're operating like a hot knife through butter. It's an effortlessness and ease of being that makes living your life a pleasure. It's living with integrity, in support of your values.

Some of us, in the deepest recesses of our soul, think, "Who am I to make decisions for myself? I'm not smart enough, thin enough, strong enough, educated enough, loved enough, or just plain enough." I ask, "Who are you not to?" You are entitled to have your own needs, preferences and feelings. Making decisions for yourself, and handling the consequences, is also your right. If you give that right away, you give away the right to create a life of your own making.

Deciding is integral to human living. Few of us are exempt. And making decisions is generally not a one-time thing. We decide about the job only to face a set of decisions about the house. We choose the school, then have to choose the major. It's a couch, then a rug. So it's important to get really, really good at it – because mastering decision-making prevents us from getting stuck in limbo land and allows us to craft a life of our own design.

Standard Operating Procedure

THE MILITARY INVENTED THE IDEA OF STANDARD OPERATING procedure. When in doubt, default to the SOP and, by taking the specified steps, your outcome will be exactly as the SOP predicts.

In my time in government, I came to think "SOP" really stood for "Same Old Plan". The Same Old Plan keeps things safe and comfortable – and the outcome predictable.

Which is OK.

But not exactly creative. Or ground-breaking. Or exciting. Or quick. Or always right. In truth, the SOP doesn't have to solve the problem – it just has to be followed.

I discovered that sometimes, in order to really solve the problem, you have to throw out the SOP in favor of a NIP. A New Innovative Plan.

To build a NIP, all you have to do is exactly the opposite of what the SOP requires. There's an old joke that goes something like this: "Man: 'Doctor, it hurts when I go like this' (banging his head against the table) Doctor: 'The cure is simple. Stop banging your head against the table.'"

Plain and simple – a NIP keeps you from banging your head against the table. Here's a helpful way to decide if you need a NIP or an SOP – if a SOP works, keep doing it. But if it's not working, NIP it in the bud. [I crack myself up.]

If your weight loss plan isn't working, take a look at your SOP. Not the SOP you tell everyone, but the SOP you actually follow, which is something like: "I'll get started on my diet tomorrow. Tonight I'm going to have this half gallon of ice cream." Remember, your NIP is the exact opposite of what you usually do, so your NIP is, "I'm starting right now and not eating the ice cream."

Want better communication with your teenager? Look at how you're communicating now. If your SOP is lectures, edicts and nagging, do you really wonder why she won't talk with you? Try the opposite – listening, asking questions and showing respect for her opinions. You may not see a cleaner room, but you'll definitely have a better relationship.

"I keep meeting the same kind of guys," says a single woman. "They're irresponsible and all they want is a good time." OK. "Where are you looking?" she's asked. "Oh, in strip clubs, off-track betting shops and at dog fights. I guess there just aren't any respectable men left." Oh, there are plenty of them – in places opposite to where you're looking. Try libraries, offices, dog parks, animal shelters, shopping malls, churches, synagogues, mosques and Buddhist meditation centers. For a start.

In the places in your life where you're stuck, take a look at your SOP. If it's not working for you, if you're not making the change you really, really want, then give a NIP a try. Do the exact opposite of what you've been doing, and watch your progress.

There's a disputed quote, attributed to both Ben Franklin and Albert Einstein, defining insanity as "doing the same thing over and over, hoping for a different outcome." In that light, following a SOP is often an insane course. The NIP, however, is a pretty sane approach, don't you think?

You can attribute that one to me.

⁓

HERE, BUT NOT HERE

THE OTHER DAY I WAS IN THE MALL RUNNING SOME ERRANDS and saw the cutest high school couple. Their arms were entwined – her right hand in his back pocket, his left in hers – as they walked arm in arm. Sweet. Brought back memories. Until I looked closer and saw that the boy was chit-chatting on his cell phone while he strolled with his sweetie. Sweetie had a look on her face which was one part "Woo-hoo! I've-got-a-boyfriend-look-at-me" and one part "When is he going to get off the phone?"

This brought to mind a trip to Disney World where I saw a father glued to his Blackberry while the family stood in a slow-moving line. The mother would try to engage him in a conversation with her and the kids and he would absently respond, "Uh, huh" or "Mmmm" whether or not those were relevant responses. Finally, the exasperated mother said, "Honey, we are on vacation. This is not your office. Put the Blackberry away." It was as if he were coming out of a trance as he slipped it into his pocket. He was there, but not there. I wonder where he wanted to be.

Cell phones and Blackberrys have given us a way to be present physically but absent, practically. We're here, but not here. And, for the sake of our relationships, I think it's time we put the phone down, so we can be right here, right now.

Now, I'm no Luddite. I don't hate technology. I like technology. In fact, I am a gadget girl. Give me a new electronic gizmo and I can spend hours noodling with it. I read about new cell phones, TVs, DVDs, computers, programs, cameras, PDAs – all that stuff. I'm an early adopter who enjoys finding new tools which allow me to do things more efficiently. Especially tools with cool little buttons that make noises and glow in the dark.

But cell phones and Blackberrys are everywhere, and steal our time and attention. They allow us to keep relationships at an arm's length (the length of the arm holding the phone, bent to our ear, in fact). They help us stay superficially involved. It's as if we're asking for credit for hanging out with one person while we're really hanging out with whoever's on the other end of the phone.

When you're there, but not there, you divide your attention so no one or nothing is getting all of you. Some of us seem to use the cell phone for precisely this reason. The distance provided by being on a call calibrates a relationship. It gives power to the person with the phone – they decide who can talk with whom, when. It provides a great excuse for emotional distance. I don't have to be fully engaged in a difficult discussion with you because (saved by the bell!) my phone is ringing!

I tell my clients, "Look at how you're spending your time and you will know where your priorities lie." What are you telegraphing about your priorities when you interrupt a conversation with a real, live person to take a call from a person who's not even there? How do you think the person you're sitting across the table from, who you've effectively put on "hold", feels? Important? Valuable? Relevant?

Take a minute to think about the times when you're there, but not there. Gizmos and gadgets can create a false urgency in our lives. They decide so you don't have to. But they can't have relationships for you.

Setting boundaries around when you answer calls, or check email, can help get you started on building quality relationships with people in your life. Need some help finding appropriate boundaries? Here are some ideas:

- No answering the phone when there's only one other person present – say your spouse, your child, your parole officer
- No checking email in church or at your child's play or during your performance review
- You might even consider – gasp – not taking your cell phone or Blackberry on vacation

"But, Michele!" you gasp. "I'm multi-tasking! Isn't that what an effective person does?"

No. Multi-tasking is when you try to cram more into a minute than a minute deserves. Multi-tasking is what an overwhelmed, overstressed, anxious person does. A balanced person, present in the moment, actually does one thing at a time, devoting as much attention as needed to accomplish the task at hand.

Now, does that mean that if you leave a message for someone you can't do a thing until they return your phone call? You certainly may do something else. But when they call you back, don't check your email while you conduct your call.

Because you'll be there, but not there.

"But, Michele!" you shout. "I'm very important! The office can't do without me! I have to be in touch 24/7! I have to have my Blackberry."

I know you are very, very important. But play a game with me, will you? Name a really important person in the world. OK – the Pope. Do you think the Pope carries a Blackberry? Does he check it during church? Does he answer his cell phone when he's having audiences? Or hearing confession?

My guess is that the Pope knows what's important. He knows the greatest gift you can give someone else is to be there with them. To hear them, to know them, to respect them, to be present right there, in that moment, with them.

The secret to happy lives and rich relationships has nothing to do with gizmos and gadgets – it has everything to do with you, and how often you can be right here, right now. Set your own priorities. Don't let some electronic device serve as an artificial barrier to meaningful connection with others.

You owe it to yourself, and others, to be here, now.

WHELMED

THE OTHER DAY A WOMAN REPORTED THAT SHE WAS FEELING overwhelmed — she was trying to do so much that she felt she wasn't doing anything well. Was multi-tasking the answer, she asked?

No, I answered, multi-tasking doesn't really work. Try mono-tasking instead. Do one thing at a time. Do it thoroughly and do it well. Then move on to the next thing. Mono-tasking.

When you're multi-tasking — trying to do two or three things simultaneously — you end up doing none of them well. Your stress level goes through the roof.

Face it, there's just one you. You have the wondrous ability to give 100% of your attention to something. Multi-tasking asks you to divide your attention, and you end up with less than 100% on each task – and this is where errors occur...you end up spending more time fixing the resulting problems than you would if you gave the task all of your attention at the start.

Reading a memo while on a conference call when researching data and preparing a Power Point – you're not truly engaged in any of these tasks and probably won't have a great result. How much better to be truly present for the one minute it takes to read the memo, then participate fully in the conference call and make time later to do thorough, comprehensive research before you design the Power Point. That seems doable, manageable and calm, doesn't it?

The opposite of overwhelmed, of course, is underwhelmed. Underwhelmed is what teachers generally feel about the work product of boys in their first year of high school. Wives are often underwhelmed by the anniversary gifts their husbands proffer — word to the wise: just because Hallmark says it's the Paper Anniversary doesn't mean paper towels are an appropriate gift. Hallmark is referring to the *wrapping paper* around the gift. Honey, every anniversary is the jewelry anniversary. That's all you need to remember.

Underwhelm is often about our expectations of what others should be doing. And you know I have a deep dislike of the word 'should'. In my life, I simply replace 'should' with 'choose' and feel so much happier. Rather than saying, "Charlie shouldn't have shopped at 7-Eleven on Christmas Eve for my gift", you can get to a level of acceptance when you realize Charlie chose to give you that box of frozen burritos — and you can ask him about that choice.

(By the way, Charlie, see above reference to The Jewelry Rule for Anniversaries. Same rule applies to Christmas. You're welcome.)

Overwhelmed. Underwhelmed. It occurred to me this week that no one ever says, "I feel whelmed." We're always over or under.

Wouldn't it be lovely to answer the question, "How you doing today?" with "I'm whelmed, thank you very much! And you?"

Whelmed — the point at which you are neither over nor under. You are not fruitlessly multi-tasking. You are balanced. You are paying appropriate attention and spending appropriate time on your tasks.

You are whelmed.

As the holidays approach with their attendant stressful opportunities for overwhelming tasks and underwhelming performance by others – reduce your stress by choosing to be whelmed. Whelmed one task at a time.

༄

Made in the USA